INGREDIENTS

IN-STRUCTIONS

Ascension is unavoidable. One cannot try to ascend, for trying causes static in the natural flow of the Universe, which is the will of God. Lucid Living is an alchemist's channel of light frequencies here to assist you in your enlightenment.

If you choose to partake in this conversation, let it guide you inward with your loving light of awareness. Do go into your darkness, but do not forget to bring your light. With an empty mind and an open heart, keep what resonates with you and disregard what does not.

May this conversation bring you inspiration, clarity, love, health, abundance and peace for the rest of your life and for every lifetime to come. May God bless eternal and infinite gratitude, generosity, humility, and all that is good unto every being who sees, reads, holds, speaks of, hears the name of, and so much as even thinks of this book. And so it is.

GRATITUDE

Gratitude to the Archangels for their sacred service.

Michael, with strength like God. Thank you for your fortitude. Free us of all forms of attachment and lower vibrational stagnation so that we may expand into our light freely sharing our spiritual gifts with the world.

Raphael, bearer of remedy. Thank you for your medicine.

Heal our wounds and afflictions now so that we may affect others with our healing.

Gabriel, bringer of faith. Thank you for your information. Deliver God's unique and divine messages to every being with eyes to see and ears to hear.

Jophiel, one of great beauty. Thank you for your light. Show us all of the peaceful magnificence of this world and beyond.

Ariel, lion of God. Thank you for protecting the earth. Keep our oceans and forests safe and bring healing to our animals.

Azreal, one who assists. Thank you for your love. Support all beings in adjustment to loss with ease and grace.

Chamuel, the seer. Thank you for your
wisdom. Show us our interconnectedness to all
living beings that we may never forget our
oneness.

1 MASTERY

Beliefs are the foundation for everything.

Every door is the gateway to enlightenment and acceptance is the skeleton key. To refuse the present circumstances is to reject happiness. There is no such thing as toxic masculinity, nor toxic femininity. There is simply toxicity, in infinitely varying degrees. Indeed, the process of boxing and labeling any form of negativity as either masculine or feminine is futile in and of itself.

Class is taking the high path beyond impression. Class does not care how it appears to others. None other but thyself could remove thy crown. For they have crowned them self. Therefore, class cares how it appears only to the one.

One can be magnificently insightful. Insightful is the ability to see both the past and the present in real time. The perfect mastery is the balance of love and discernment. By focusing on the gold, one may let the past make them better, not bitter.

There are so many things that could have happened differently. Yet in order for one to make the present perfect, they must make the past perfect in their mind. For it is the past that has brought them to the present moment. That is to say, get real with how ye feeleth, so ye can healeth.

One may not see how this present moment is perfect, and by releasing attachment to all expectations, then the present moment will be made perfect naturally. Even just for this moment. It is not in letting go of expectations, but in letting go of the attachment to expectations that awakens the deepest power within them. It is the perfect practice; for it is the practice that makes perfect.

In order to build high, one must first build out. Only by surrounding one's self with positive people may they keep on a positive trajectory. Only by remaining positive may they keep surrounded by positive people. It is the youinverse.

Beliefs are the codes to reality. People change their reality by changing their beliefs. A reality is simply a system of beliefs. The beliefs one holds about their parents become the realities of one's life. To change their life, one may change the beliefs they hold about their parents. To change the current circumstances, one must change their beliefs about the current circumstances.

By changing one's beliefs, they change the entire situation. Beliefs are the foundation for everything. Beliefs are the building blocks that hold the matrix together. Don't just stand there and stoop, rise up and transmute. What thou art seeking is seeking thee, so let it come. Rumi.

The naysayers are the ones who work for the

darkness. Because they don't believe in themselves, they won't believe in thee. Because they can't find their love, they won't see thy light.

As a person ages, they begin to realize that nothing matters in life as much as how lovingly they love. It's always best to have good will towards everyone, because one cannot control others, but one may control them self to the extent of their awareness. Awareness is the skeleton key. Awareness dissolves all barriers. Awareness broadens the only path.

At times it will feel like people are out of line, but once one has begun to awaken, they start to realize there is no line. It doesn't matter if it feels like people are out of line, it is always best to be kind. Careful is not fear based, care full is love based.

One only knows what they love by knowing themselves, and they come to know the self, by taking risks. For it is in their responses to fear, that one comes to the self.

Lies are lonely. A reality built on lies is like a house of cards, it crumbles with pressure. Truth is faith. A house build of faith becomes a mountain. Mountains may move, but they remain forever, even under water. One cannot be both a leader and a people pleaser at the same time, thou must choose. In a wolf pack, the alpha does not lead the pack, the alpha stands 100 feet back from the sick and elderly to ensure the entire pack is safe.

Temper is a person's Achilles heel. One is only as good as their temperament. One who can control their temper, can do anything. Anger is the fire of protection, if not contained it will burn a person's life to the ground, and they may lose everything in it. Anger is often the result of the best intentions, and shines light on the trigger points of a person's greatest weakness.

Often times there is good reason to be angry, but always there is better reason to remain calm. It is because the masculine has fought and killed for hundreds of generations. Only recently has the masculine begun to step into healing, and that is a good thing.

All beings are on their own journey, even unto love. When thou stops taking things personal, everyone becomes beautiful. Rich means potent in goodness; one can have no money and be rich. One may have all the money in the world and be poor, and broke. Rich is a mindset; it means I have more than I need.

Death does not happen in an instant, it happens over a lifetime and only takes an instant. The wise practice dying daily, by focusing on the light. If only people knew that they could be whatever they choose, their success in being has nothing to do with the validation or perception of others. Seeing only the good in everything leads some people to put their defenses down. Walking with their defenses down makes it easier for others to hurt them. The pain makes them stronger, so they can hold their defenses

8

up, but not so high that they cannot see.

One must move slowly to win the walk of life, for if they move too quickly all the spectators will miss them. The walk of life is judged by the spectators yet accompanied by friends. One honors them back, that they not become a spectator. It is honor and respect that creates leaders.

Do not be fueled by the media, do not be fooled by the tricks. The maytricks does not want people to know their greatest power thrives in humility.

An individual will be the only person who sees their own dream for a period of time. If they remain loyal to holding that vision, eventually another person will see their dream too. If they keep holding it, eventually 2, then 4, then more will see their dream.

The more people that realize one's dream, the more their dream becomes realeyesed. People become what the psychic support of the collective see. Support the collective, and they will support thee. The world is thy reflection, truly… the world is a reflection of you.

The world is a stage. Nature is the truth. The world is a play. Nature is the script. The world is full of actors. Nature is the music. Hatred is fears attempt at appearing brave. Do not let the hatred of others frighten you, realize that those who hate thee are more afraid of thee than thou art of them.

If one can be anything, then they can be anything, so allow thyself to be anything. Because one is patient, they wait for things to align completely before taking action. Because they wait for things to be aligned completely before taking action, one is successful.

One can only be as successful as they can be patient. Discipline is the key to patience, and patience is the doorway to success. Success happens over the course of a lifetime, but it witnessed in an instant. It took years to develop electricity, but it was over night that the world came to experience it.

2 HEAVEN

Heaven (have in) is within you.

Gratitude is the gateway to heaven, generosity is the key, and humility is the path. Heaven, have in, is within you. Everyone comes from the light, thus everyone sees light when they pass on to the other side, because they are moving into and coming from a new light.

If one's vibration is not preconditioned to the requisite understanding of oneness, they won't resonate in alignment with the higher light realm and will timelessly move through, rebirthed by portals of lower light realm vibration. Each new rebirthing is the same soul, with a new body and thus a different spirit. As one's vibration aligns with heavenly frequencies on the Earthly plane, they are enabled to remain in higher light realm planes sharing life with the same soul family as shared with in the lower light realm. Heaven is a term for higher dimension, each new higher dimensional plane is a form of heaven. The ascension is infinite. The descension can also be infinite. They are one.

For, oneness is the substance of heaven. This soul may remain in Utopia until called back to lighter light realm by source for the sake of the expansion of oneness.

Oversouls evolve through identical processes, and so-on up the lineage, lineage, into the light, until soul reaches source and returns home. This process feels like eternity for just one soul, it is eternity for all of soul, for everything is infinity, but soul cannot feel that eternity while encapsulated into a physical vessel countless lower light realm portals away from source. The body will either ascend or it will perish. Upon perishing all of its light is assembled in the Ajna and beamed upward through the higher light portals towards source where it is downloaded with new light codes necessary for its next descent. If, however, the body ascends, all of its light will expand "outwardly" (inwardly) through every atom of its being towards source, vanishing from lower light realm and becoming one with all that is. This is the ascension and is as easy as levitating.

People love to watch a fire burn. If one is not reverent towards the lives of others, they become the fire. Many light beings here hold the giant fire down from massive consumption. The good become the light, the not good become the darkness. Do not fear entering into the realm of darkness. The fire is karma, the light is consciousness. Darkness is the lack of consciousness. As thou would not fear what ye already understand, so thee should not fear the darkness, but seek to understand it. When one looks into the fire, the oversoul experiences karma, and descension ensues, for the flame is consuming.

The pendulum swings, into infinity, always expanding equally into all directions. Smiles turn to tears, as the happier one gets, the sadder they become. The unpeeling of layers. We must not resist feelings of discomfort but move through them. The things one possessed began to end up possessing them, so they gave their things away to those in need. And now they are no longer in need. They became free, by freeing everything else. Now they have space to see.

One is on a path to heaven, held in such a high light by others, due to what they saw. One's decisions become their vibration. Ye vibration is held in place by the perspective of thy surroundings, as well as thyself. So, give no one a reason to despise thee, simply allow karma to do its work. If ye give no one a reason to despise thee and they do it anyway, thy angels will pluck them from thine field.

People exist in the center of perspective; thus, life is a reflection. By keeping balance, they remain at the fulcrum point of peace. Going too quickly in one direction or another is to ascend or descend through extreme decisions, by taking extreme risks. Slow and steady wins the race, as they say. "Grown ups" have grown up problems. If ye want to grow, pick up a problem. If thou don't want to grow up, have no problems. Only in the mind do problems exist, for God, the Universe, or whatever you choose to call it knows what it is doing.

As children we were taught to believe in a white bearded man who knows when we have been good and knows when we have been bad. Who sees us when we are sleeping, and blesses us for being good, but punishes us for being bad with coal. Coal is the result of something having been burnt to ash, such as the fires of hell. In coming to realize that Santa Clause does not exist, the void was filled with a new white bearded man who also lives in the sky, or Northern most pole, and is always watching to make sure they are doing the right thing; Eye call this the Santa Clause Complex.

Here is the truth, no one is watching you but you. And you are connected to everything that is, so everything is watching you.

People don't do things, their over soul does things for them. People are simply along for the ride, but if they try too hard, they block the path. Integrity is connecting with thy oversoul, the higher self. Limiting beliefs and laziness is connecting with the under soul; the lower self. Did thou think thee had a higher self but not a lower self? This is how the lower self remains in control, by staying incognito. Remain strong in faith, by always looking towards the light, all ways up. Even in singing, only go deep to vibrate out all that does not serve thee.

14

The universe, tests you to see if thou will commune with thy oversoul or thine under soul. The tests always continue to grow, as ye do, all the way into infinity. One need not do anything but be one. Balance is to not overextend or take leaps too large. Giant leaps get people where they are trying to go faster, but where there is rush there is also crash. Balance is Utopia. The now is Utopia. In Utopia all is perfectly symmetrical and one. Rather than trying to go somewhere, simply come here. Utopia is the Garden of Eden, the fulcrum point of light and dark. Once out of alignment, Utopia ends for the awareness. Utopia is where nothing is overly ecstatic, and nothing is overly dramatic. That which is overly ecstatic is bound to attachment. But detachment is the key to Utopia. Balance is the key to enlightenment. Yoga is a practice of balance. Life is also a practice of balance. Life is yoga.

One wants everyone to hear the news, until they realize it is actually true. The realness of the truth places people into the seat of their soul. The aware do not alarm the asleep. We sing them into love.

Family are the closest of souls. The family members one vibrates best with are closest to them in higher light realm. The family members one is most at odds with, are closest to them in lower light realm. Higher light realm souls bless one as they descend.

Lower light realm souls scorn one as they

ascend. This is why one turns the other cheek, it's for ascension. One turns the other cheek for them self. For if one engages with the darkness upon ascent, they are pulled back.

If an innocent being shall remain in a place of reverence, even unto harm, they shall ascend. The light and the dark are pulling for thy awareness, both at the same time. Ye will follow the direction thou look. Look into the love of friendship, and away from the judgment of media. The light wants to pull thee up, its strength depends on whether or not thou feed it with thought. Life happens so fast, in every moment thou art the decision. There is no moment to spare, everything one does, can be done for others. Every moment between every second is a cascade into a new reality. It happens so fast most miss it.

Affirm the life of thy highest desire by choosing thy posture, choosing thy words, and choosing thy actions purposefully. Everyone who receives can be grateful and everyone who can be grateful receives, the choice is thine. Those who are not grateful are missing what they are receiving. Those who are not grateful experience descension. Those who are not generous do not understand giving, and they scorn those who give. Those who are selfish think only for themselves, this is not oneness. Oneness is love. Love is the mortar of heaven.

To break the body is to break the mind. The mind can repair, but only with body re-alignment. Body work is one of the top 3 most sacred of services.

Along with music, and medicine. With these three services the body, mind and soul are able to be unified. Body work can also be energy work, for the body is actually only energy.

Nobody is missing anything. Yet everyone says, "I miss" you, without realizing this is a spell. Thou art whole and complete, always. It is simple enough to say, "I love you", but to say you are missing something is to confirm an affirmation of lack, affirm abundance. The beginning of depression is the start of awakening. The new game is more challenging than the last, but only at first.

The brain is an ascension device; a calculator. The brain is the body, not just a mass of cells compartmentalized in the cranium. The heart is also the brain, as well as the stomach, and so on. The brain is a navigation device. Thou art traveling the ether with it right now, in thine merkaba, or light body. Care for thy vessel so that it can hold high frequency without tearing thine merkaba. Fortunately, one may repair a damaged merkaba, but this world contains frequencies that will leave holes in one's vessel; electromagnetic frequencies and radiations.

We are developing tools for shielding those forms of electronic warfare. Such as ormus and carbon 60.

As with all tools, one must educate them self before using them. One cannot pick up a gun without knowing what it is and try to use it, the first thing they'd do is look into the barrel and pull the trigger. So, educate thyself, before following thy surroundings.

When one finally realizes how much their over soul family is doing to support their destiny, it may humble him into tears. All destiny is beautiful, and all family is one. Our decisions effect each other's vibrations on a metaphysical level.

Every decision is a cascade. It is by loyalty to the virtues that ascension is made possible. It is lonely at the top because people are afraid to reach up. But it is not lonely at the top because there are high beings waiting for thee. Let go of the past. People are not afraid of rejection; they are afraid of ascension. It is change they fear and limiting beliefs that keep their fears alive. But truly, alone is all one.

Everything and everyone is a form of the matrix. Because one is the matrix, as one changes, so will their matrix. The walls of the matrix are built of their synapses. They enter into the matrix by entering into their own subconscious mind. Alchemy and meditation allow for timeline hopping through portals, and that is how new realities are constructed.

Decisions are doorways into new realities.

Food is a portal into a new dream. Life is thy dream.

Every time one makes the right decision, they enter a new reality. It is not before long that they realize life has changed, and so have the people in it.

Every single thought is an entirely new portal. Upon attaching to a thought one steps into a new world. The further they step into that new world, the more tangible and real that world becomes. Choose loving thoughts, always.

The virtues are decisions, and the sins are decisions too. The darkness is clever, but the light feels better.

One continues to ascend by making the right decisions. To do the right thing is to think the right thought, is to choose love, is to look towards the light, is to ascend, is to live an upgraded dream, is to experience a more fruitful life, is to have higher quality relationships. It all leads to oneness.

Sometimes, before things can be upgraded, those things must crumble. A dream cannot live on the foundation of a nightmare. So do not fear chaos. Understand that chaos is the groundwork for a new dream. Everything is a giant screen.

There is no one to truly trust but trust itself. Have faith in faith. First, thou must trust in thyself, in order to trust in others. And one cannot truly trust in them self when they only use about 10% of their own brain, and even their own brain is 90% foreign matter. The individuals self is about .1% of their being, so we must trust in God, the universe, the whole. Everything and everyone is an extension of the self, we are everything. So simply trust. Do not trust in him, or her, or anything. Just trust in trust. With but the faith of a mustard seed. Faith and doubt cannot co-exist. All it takes is the faith of a mustard seed, because wherever there is even a seed of faith, there can be no doubt.

One can gracefully let go of the people they lost, and warmly welcome the people who come. Every story they tell, is a doorway to a new portal. A portal for himself.

Purgatory is the void, the space between the dreams. Purgatory is where time stops, and one makes a choice; love or fear. Always choose love. All ways.

By digging into one's own mind, they are able to discover the programs that operate their beingness. By discovering the programs, one may delete, reconfigure, and rearrange his belief systems. Control + Alt + Delete. Reconfigure using more positive codes to live a better life.

Needing is only around when one wants something they cannot have. There is no time for need when one is so filled with gratitude, and without need there is no crime. Only when one needs something they cannot have; do they want to do something they can not do. Cognitive split ensues. To want something that is meant for occurrence is not needing but is inspiration. The wanting of something one can not have is the cause of procrastination and stagnation. Thus, one who hesitates is lost.

One who follows a distraction, enters into a lower vibrational dream, otherwise known as a nightmare. One who stays on course, remains constantly entering into a more beautiful dream, otherwise known as lucid.

3 YOUINVERSE

Without that which is not, there can be
no that which is.

Be as a lion in a world of dogs, as a dog in
a world of chickens, and a chicken in a world
of worms. No matter who thou art, thou art
exquisite and powerful. How doest thou view
thyself, whether one thinks they are powerful
or not, they are still powerful. One may just
not know their own power. A Ferrari without
wheels is still a Ferrari, it just can't go
anywhere. Equip thyself with wheels of faith.

Remember thou art divine. There is always
something more, or less, but worship what
thou art and thou shall naturally blossom like a
golden lotus flower. Do not be a chicken and
wish thou were a lion, be a chicken happy thou
art not a worm. Think it, speak it, write it, be
it, and it is done.

The key to productive action is self-
confidence. If one does not believe they can do
it, they will only try. If one believes they can
do it, it will be done. In changing one's self

they change the entire world. No person can change another. No person can teach another, each person can make the choice to see and to hear for themselves.

Allow everything in existence to be thy teacher. The loud neighbor that throws parties until 5am, the competitor that slanders, the disease, even the parasite; let it all teach. It is all hear to teach thee. In receiving the lessons of obstacles, thou maketh blessings.

People can only know what they have seen. We must show those who pity themselves what power looks like, by not playing into their victim mentality.

If they choose to remain where they are, feeling sorry for themselves and angry towards others, then leave them there for what they truly need is enough time with themselves until they can no longer live with themselves and must change. Deathbed wishes become future lives, be careful for what thou wish for, whilst closing thou eyes.

While drifting off to sleep, keep positive mantras in thy mind, that thou may move through portals into high light realm in thy sleep. More than 99.9% of every atom is space, and an exponentially greater amount of space exists between the atoms. Everything is made up of atoms. Thy body art space. What lives within that space is energy, inner-g. God. Which is everything thou see.

One's body is not confined to the third dimension. The energy living within all lives through and within all of life in this universe, moving through all things at a singular point of time which is present in both past, future, now and all possible versions of this holy trinity.

The Akashtic records are contained within thy DNA. DNA moves through space and attaches to all that is, for there are infinite strands unmeasurable by the linear technologies of today. Atlantis had quantum technologies to measure multi-dimensional conditions, so we know it can be done, but those technologies are hidden from us today. We must remember.

Classifications of energy are made possible by the identification of freequency. Frequent seas of wavelength. Frequency is what differentiates the infinite spectrum of energy wavelength from one form to another. That frequency is information destined to be articulated by the computer, that is thy mind, into a story. This is how with our consciousness we create the world. If a tree falls in the woods and no one is around to hear it, does it make a sound? If no one is around, there are no woods.

Tesla said something along the lines of, "If you want to understand the universe think in terms of frequency, energy and vibration". Something similar was stated by Albert Einstein; "Energy can never be destroyed nor created, it only changes form". In the bible, God is written to have spoken the following words, "I am the Alpha and Omega. The beginning and the end. The first and the last". - Rev 22:13 In science it is proven that energy can never be destroyed, nor created, but can only change forms. It would seem then that God, therefore, is energy; all that is, and all that ever was. If energy moves through all things, then God moves through all things. This means that to not worship anything is to not worship God. So, then worship is to give praise for that which we see, and what we see resides within. Reverent is to see the sacred in all things, this is Godly.

One must honor all things as God if they are to honor them self. Truly, the only way to honor one's self is to honor all things. There is no separation.

The goodness of one's life is directly

proportional to the selflessness of their thoughts. Yes, we fill our cup until it overflowed. But we only fill our cup so that the overflow may fill others. We do not fill our cup until it overfloweth and then attempt to catch our own overflow, one would drop and break their cup that way.

Nothing causes more telomere shortening, and cellular death than stress. Except for possibly 5G radiation, which is why Ormus Carbon 60 is essential for this time period. Carbon 60 removes oxidative stress from the body, before it damages the DNA. Oxidative stress is caused by both internal and external factors, but internal factors are largely in thy control. Think of it this way, one will stay as young as they are positive. If one routinely thinks negative thoughts about anything or anyone, then they are an assassin unto their self. If ye hold a grudge against anyone, just tell them how thee feel and move on with thy life. That, or give it to God.

But one who goes through life stewing on sabotaging or in any other way wishing harm to another, only harms themself. Do not harm thy brothers, leave thy poison on the shelf. Do not harm thy sister, even if thou think thou art stealth. Negativity only destroys the cells of one's own self.

One can only understand life to the extent that they understand energy, for life is energy. Life is not the color of one's skin, their social class, or gender. Rather, life is the thoughts that one emits regarding these things; race, gender, society, self, and so on... anti-thoughts are anti-life. If one thinks positive thoughts, they lead a good life. It's simple, but people have forgotten.

Since energy has always been and will always be, it holds within it the blueprint of all things that have ever been and ever will be, and all things hold within it one energy. God, the Alpha and Omega, the beginning and end, the Omni Valent, knowing all things, Energy... so many names.

But the Universe does not define God because God is far more vast than the Universe, and even the Universe is far more enormous than the Universe as we know it. There are about 600 races of extra-terrestrial that do trade with the human race on earth, about 600 billion other earth like planets in the Milky Way, over 500 million other galaxies in our universe, and other worlds beyond our universe, which is just one tiny bubble surrounded by grander bubbles. Some people think as if they are the center of the earth, and as if the earth is the center of the

Universe. Actually, all points are the center, there is no one center; there is but one. Everything is a sphere. Humility is truth, pride is fraudulent.

Virtually, thou have access to everything. God does not judge, because God is the isness of that which would have been judged. All things that exist have God within them, and God has all things that exist within it. Judgment is lack of understanding.

Judge not, for all things are God's creation. To judge God's creation would be to judge God, and to assume that God does not know what it is doing. If God does not know what it's doing, then nothing knows what it's doing, therefore there would be no right or wrong and thus, nothing to judge anyway. And if God does know what it's doing, then everything happens for a divine purpose far greater than the human mind can comprehend, and so still there is nothing to judge. Either way, there is nothing to judge. But if one should choose to stand in judgment and destroy themselves, that is where they are at along their journey and we can let them stay there.

One's faith is proven by their state of acceptance. Faith is the greatest of all power. Compassion is truth, truth is understanding.

That which understands does not judge. People only judge what they do not understand. Judgment is the evidence of ignorance. Where there is judgment, there is ignorance. One who condemns others hates that which they condemn within themself. One who blames others neglects that part of themself.

The word "Goddess" implies that God is gender specific. God is all encompassing; God is not gender specific. To give gender energy is to impose a division upon life. The masculine and the feminine are one, like the yin yang. There is no yang without yin, and there is no yin without yang. That is why it is not the yin and yang; it is the yin yang.

We were brought here to unify the masculine and the feminine, not to amplify division by stepping even further into gender expectations.

There is no need to say "he" when referring to God. When referring to God, it is simply enough to say, "God". God is already a name. God is the name for energy, and energy is the name for everything that is, so there is no need to give God a name. One could say it, for "it" or "I" for God is that "I am, that I am" consciousness that is all things, including me and thee.

This is why I speak in terms of One-ness. And why I equate one to them, because as above so below. One who worships all things as their self truly worships God. Elohim is an ancient translation for the word God. Elohim was both male and female. These ancients believed that feminine is form and masculine is consciousness.

A belief is not necessarily a truth but can be true. A belief is true to the extent that it pertains to time and space in bringing peace to all beings. The measurement of truth is how many beings it brings peace to. Unconditionally honesty is not always the most diplomatic course of action while dealing with highly sensitive beings who have not yet learned to take nothing personal. Therefore, there is a difference between truth and honesty. True is Gods standards, honest is thy standards. One who aligns their honesty with God's truth, speaks the truth. One can only speak the truth to the extent that they understand energy. Become one with energy, that is to let go of judgement, to transcend thy mind.

They say the left side of the body is the feminine, the receiving side. The right side of the body is the masculine, the giving side. Adam being first, the "atom", building block of all form in the material realm. These ancients believed that matter was feminine, and consciousness was masculine. By using consciousness, one may shape matter, or at least shift it. Masculinity which protects the feminine is protected by God. For the feminine is matter, all forms of matter, according to those ancient. The man who serves the feminine is blessed by the universe. If there was no matter, there would be no way for consciousness to experience itself. If there was no consciousness there would be no life in the matter.

The Atlantean Law states that women respect their brothers as their sisters and men respect their sisters as their brothers. All beings are both masculine and feminine. Some beings more extreme examples of this, such as the African Reed Frog who can fluctuate from being male or female depending on environmental factors and the needs of procreation.

By worshipping the feminine, man brings honor to God. The feminine can be a storm, but man must not be shaken, and his ability to withstand the storm is evidence to his true masculinity, or so they say.

However, it is best to transmute all gender

expectations in general and simply refocus the aim on what it means to be a good and loving person. Atlantis did not hold gender expectations. That is how Atlantis kept peace. Both men and women are warriors, lovers, space holders, and raisers of children.

There is no need to use words like priestess or Goddess because priest and God are not masculine or gender specific terms. Only by adding ess to God and priest do people impose division between genders, division is destabilization, but men and women are not meant to be divided.

Yet ess has been added to the term God because people began referring to God as "he". This was not so in the original texts. God is not "he"; God is "God". A priest is a priest, a God is a God, regardless of whether they are man or woman.

4 HAPPINESS

Acceptance is the key to forgiveness.

A body must be capable of holding a frequency in order for that body to be experienced by the awareness moving through it. By shaping one's body to hold high frequency, one may experience more of the positive feelings and less of the negative feelings. The body is a transmuting temple.

Oneness is freedom. One may raise their frequency by detaching from things. Things are objects, people, and ideas. The more things one detaches from, the more they become one again, that is to say one with everything.

Information moves through space and is perceived by itself, as it interacts with components of itself that are separated through the void. Light can observe itself by interacting with darkness, and darkness can observe itself by interacting with light. This is why the light and darkness both need and love each other.

Life is a game, and the game does not exist without both. Light cannot judge the darkness, or else it would become the darkness. Thus, judge not lest ye be judged. The evidence of darkness is judgment. The Darkness can become the light through love. Love behaves like gratitude, generosity and humility.

If one seeks to make the biggest change in the world, they may go into the darkness, and then love everything. They will illuminate the darkness. That is what the fiercest of spiritual warriors do. That is why they are considered worries. They slay their own demons, with love. And those demons do not die, they are transmuted into the light worries as fierce in magnitude as they were in the darkness. The darkness is confusing, and consuming.

Thus, the darkness uses lies as a tool to recruit. It is the confusion that leads people off the path. But truly, light is not the path, light is life. Darkness is the only path; darkness is the path away from life. To be in healing, and in medicine is not to be on a path. For healing and medicine are substances life is made of. Sometimes people simply experience temporary amnesia and are swayed away from life onto a separate path; one of ego, and that is darkness.

In light the ego serves thee, but in darkness ye serve the ego. The ego is not going anywhere, until the body does, but one must know how to work with it. The ego is simply an idea, it can steer a person or a person can steer it. Awakening is learning to steer the ego, rather than letting the ego steer thee.

One may intentionally enter the darkness, for the sake of illumination. Once they enter the darkness however, it is easy to forget why they are there. Then the thoughts of the darkness can play tricks on them, making them believe that others are bad and they are good.

This is why some sections of the spiritual community are self-righteous. Self-righteousness is the oldest trick in the ego's book. Light beings set their intention to illuminate the darkness and the darkness hears this. When they start getting deep into their spiritual work and seeing positive shifts, the ego starts saying to them, "Look at all this amazing work you are doing to illuminate the darkness. You should be proud. You are like a modern Jesus (or Mary). You are a savior". A phenomenon eye call Savior Fever.

The ego knows that where there is a savior there must also be a victim, and where there is a victim there must be a villain. The ego survives on these archetypes. Unconsciously, those with savior fever create villains and victims rather than creating true healing and empowerment through understanding and oneness. They fall in lust with the feeling of being holier than thou and forget that the key to happiness is service.

During their ego driven descent they succumb to judgment and condemnation rather than rising to forgiveness and compassion. Within their cults they monger of fear towards people or groups outside of their cult as a means of bonding with their followers. This is the divide and conquer ego mechanism.

Hatred is fear's attempt at appearing brave.

People only hate what they fear bears more power than them. Judgment is an act of ignorance, for people only judge what they cannot comprehend.

To insult is the act of jealousy, and jealousy is the expression of self-doubt. Self-confidence does not resist jealousy. Self-confidence feels jealousy and breaths it through with acceptance.

Hot on savior fever, these people attract wounded individuals into their groups by portraying themselves as gurus and enable those people to feel like victims who are in need of healing. Instead, they could be using their power to guide people towards personal accountability, reminding all people that our realities are the stories we tell ourselves; this is empowerment rather than victimization.

Some with savior fever start calling psychedelics medicines and overprescribe them like psychiatrists over prescribe pharmaceuticals. Once they begin journeying every weekend the ego becomes stronger. They proceed to calling molly and ketamine ascension tools. In their psychedelically enhanced state, the subconscious mind has unraveled and opened, thus the voice of every entity that has led them astray in the first place becomes even louder. Their following makes them appear as credible even though they can lie without even knowing it.

Those with savior fever might come out of a psychedelic ceremony thinking they have enlightened and start selling themselves as embodiments of the divine masculine, or divine feminine, selling energy healings and life advice as if they are psychologists. Yet often they have no psychological training whatsoever other than the Landmark Forum they took one summer.

Those with savior fever do not know they operate this way. They are in need of more healing than their clients. It is the more blind leading the less blind into deeper states of blindness.

Good advice is not attaching to someone's drama, embodying the savior role, and condemning another as a villain.

Life advice is freeing them from their victimhood. Wisdom is reminding people that everything happens for them, and guiding people back towards them self. There is a silver lining in every sliver of pain. We are only strong to the extent that we have been hurt.

But it's not just cult leaders that operate by the Savior Delusion, friends and family members use fear and condemnation to keep members attached to their group also. Some clicks of friendships and families are actually cults. A cult is simply short for the word culture. Within every click is a cult.

As a rule of thumb, know that anyone who condemns another as a villain is confused by the ego and either taking the stance of a victim or a savior.

A true guru is not someone who uses condemnation to empower victim stories, but someone who uses love to awaken self-empowerment. A guru is not someone who tells one how to live their life, or what to think, but someone who shows them how to find their own voice and intuition. A GURU is not a word, it's an acronym. G(gee) U(you) R(are) U(you).

Do not be led astray by darkness in the self-righteous, just love everyone unconditionally. Even if it does not feel right, unconditional love is always the answer. Unconditional love does not mean togetherness or sex. Unconditional love means understanding and compassion.

A relationship is based on conditions, but the love of the relationship does not need to be based on conditions. Even a married couple can divorce and never speak again, but still have unconditional love, and wish the best for one another. In the same way, have unconditional love for everyone, even the politicians.

Those we know of as empaths often stay in relationships with those who have been labeled as narcissists. It's a spiritual choice. Because the empathy knows they should love unconditionally, but what the empath doesn't know is that love does not require close proximity.

No person is an empath or a narcissist, realistically, but these roles appear real. People live within unpleasant roles to remember who they are and why they came here. If one has not forgotten, then one has no need to remember. But if one forgets, only love can bring them home through forgiveness and understanding. But on a deeper level of understanding, love is home. Love is what you are.

Wounds cause people to behave in ways that may attract love, in ways that allow them to be forgiven and understood. For it was in being judged and misunderstood that they became wounded in the first place.

Wounds need love to heal, and once people heal, they begin to heal others. It's better to heal a person than condemn them, for healing one person is healing 100 people. And those 100 people go on to heal 100 more people each. Healing 1 person is healing 10,000 people. But those 10,000 people go on to heal 100 people each, so healing 1 person is healing 1,000,000, and so on... The darker the person healed; the more people will be healed by their healing. Potential is potential. One who has extreme potential for darkness also contains within them extreme potential for light. Potential is potential. Rather than seeking to destroy those thou deem consumed by darkness, seek to transmute them, illuminating the world.

All beings are wounded here. One cannot live on Earth without being wounded, that is not the soul's point of coming here. If one was not wounded, they would not be here. Every person on this planet experiences the same frequencies, but in different magnitudes, and they all handle them in their own unique way.

The need for remembrance stems from

fragmentation, which is the result of pain. Pain stores in the body and vibrationally manifests unpleasant and traumatic situations in order to catalyze an awakening.

In this way, pain is a guide, an usher into greater states of happiness than were possible before that pain came along. Those who have been hurt tend to recreate the same situations until they go inward with the light of reverence and truly face their demons rather than perpetually projecting them outward onto others. Sometimes the situations they recreate did not happen, except in their mind as a projection of their traumatic past. There is a fine line between perspective and occurrence. One should not discredit another's perspective, but one should also take all perspectives with a grain of salt. But pain presents two options; to reject the self, or to love the self.

If love is chosen the wound is healed. Should one heal all of their wounds, they would ascend and return home. Therefore, nothing happens to thee, everything happens for thee.

Pain is an usher into greater states of awareness. And awareness is the key to all things. Thank pain for showing up and being present with thee here in this life.

Life is for the sake of love, the force that holds all things together. By worshiping love's nature, one brings honor to their own nature.

The difference between happiness and pleasure is that pleasure is a feeling, and all feelings are fleeting.

Happiness is a decision, not fleeting, but a constant state of being.

Happiness is not a feeling but is the ability and decision to be present and grateful with one's emotional and external circumstances.

Pleasure is of the senses; thus, pleasure is as fickle as it is great. The senses are emotional responses to stimulation. Emotion is as meaningless as it is impactful. As impulsive as the weather, emotions are literally tied with the weather. For we are not separate from nature.

One who chases only pleasure will run them self to exhaustion, with nothing to show for their efforts, except for memories forgotten. One who bases their happiness on pleasure will forever be stuck in the pursuit of happiness, even if they win, they are lost.

Eternal happiness is to be content with what one has, what they don't have, where they are, where they are not, and with what they are becoming while still expanding towards improvement. The key to happiness is service. One can have almost everything yet be unhappy, but one can have almost nothing yet be happy.

One can be in emotional pain, and still be happy. If one finds happiness in the presence of pain, the misery leaves and power takes its place.

Happiness is the decision to be content with one's circumstances, whereas pleasure is the result of an internal or external state change, which is pleasing to the senses.

Those who live for pleasure tend to experience dynamic pendulum swings often classified as "bi-polar" tendencies. Ormus brings balance by harmonizing these polarities.

Some are extremely happy while receiving pleasure, then extremely uncomfortable while not receiving pleasure, because the pleasure is addicting. Pleasure is the beginning of all addiction.

Pleasure is to lust, as happiness is to love. Comfort is on the same end of the spectrum as pleasure. Content is on the same end of the spectrum as happiness. One can be eternally happy once they have become content with being uncomfortable. Comfort is the enemy of greatness. So the two addictions which cause the most misery are pleasure and comfort. All other addictions stem from the root of pleasure and comfort. Pleasure and comfort are the seeds to addiction.

Pleasure is the trigger of immediate gratification, and comfort is the sensation of the illusion of bliss. One may feel comfortable for a moment, but that moment does not last, in the meantime they are not growing, and time is moving on.

Some people confuse love with pleasure. Everyone loves pleasure but pleasure itself is not love. Loving pleasure is not the same as loving the things that bring pleasure. On the contrary, people think they need the things that bring them pleasure, and need is the antithesis of love. A person may think they are in love with someone who is harmful to them because they love the moments of pleasure that person brings outside of the moments of harm. In that case it is not the person they love, but the pleasure. Comfort feels gentle yet has more control over people than anything else. Both pleasure and comfort will destroy those who need them.

If one should place a frog in a hot pot of water the frog immediately jumps out. But if one should place a frog in a comfortable pot of water and then turn the heat up, the frog will stay in the water while it slowly heats and begins to boil, until it dies in that water; eye call this the Frog Trap.

People can be grateful to those who have hurt them, for those who hurt you trigger you to grow and change. Like a frog leaping out of a hot pot of water.

In some cases, the most comfortable pose the greatest threat to thy growth. And growth is happiness, for it is natural. The universe is in a constant state of expansion, and so should we be for we are all internal reflections of the universe.

Most people end up resenting what they need because need is a limitation to free will, and free will is everyone's birthright. This is how codependent relationships form from need and end in resentment.

The mind, body, and soul will remain in harmony for one who remains loyal to their service. For service is the key to happiness.

Peace awaits those in the place where the desire to know is replaced with the desire to grow. Knowing is not growing. Rather than seeking desire, seek to inspire. Positivity is reality; negativity is only a lie with real consequences.

One cannot manifest anything productive while in seek mode. Manifestation of productivity happens while in have mode. People who are grateful for what they have, while staying mindful of what they need, receive more of what they want, and less of what their soul did not come here to experience.

What one thinks about, they attract. It's as simple as that. But people process thousands of bits of information per second, so many people are not aware of what they are thinking about. External stimuli becomes subconscious thought. Be very mindful of what ye watch and listen to. Do not listen to anything or watch anything that is not made with love.

If someone has made you angry, know that the anger was already there. The person you think made you angry just showed you the anger you had been walking around with for far too long.

The person didn't "make" you angry, they only pointed a mirror at the anger hiding inside of you, hitchhiking. One ye thought made ye angry is thine angel, and ye shalt celebrate them.

Acceptance is the key to forgiveness. If one can look inward, they will find the part of them self they have not been loving. Their anger came from inside, it did not come from another person.

It doesn't make sense for one to blame anyone for their own anger, not even to blame them self.

Anger in itself is a being, a life form. If one has anger living inside of their temple, they are the one who opened the door and let anger in. By blaming someone else, one keeps the anger inside of them. That's what anger wants. But by taking responsibility, one is able to remove the anger from their sacred vessel; their holy temple.

5 ENLIGHTENMENT

God resides in the moments between the
seconds.

Follow thy heart even if it angers some people. If
thou hast angered someone it's probably because thy
light has triggered their darkness, and that's a good
thing. If thou are not making anyone mad, thou are
probably not doing anything that matters (mad-ers).

What makes a person divine is the ability to see a
weaker being, and the willingness to give them
strength. It's not just the ability, but also the
willingness.

Being able is not enough; one must will their
abilities into action. Thou art thy actions, not thy
abilities. Abilities are simply thy potential; action is
thy kinetic. Thou art feeling, and thy actions are the
cause of thy feelings. Even a thought is an action.

A thought is the decision to engage with or attach
to a certain idea. Some people do not realize that
thoughts are their free will, they think that thoughts
are the truth and that they must act on their thoughts.
No, thoughts are options, and thou must choose them
wisely, for once thou choose thy thoughts will act on
thee.

The human mind is like the iceberg. Over 99.9% of thoughts are subconscious; eye call this the Iceberg Principle. One may program their self consciously, by consistently nourishing their senses with positive messages from all around their environment. Choose thy environment based on the person thy wish to become, for programming is inevitable.

No person can block their subconscious mind, which is over 99% of the thought bank, from external stimuli depositing into their thought bank. The more negative or dark information that is deposited into thy thought bank from thy outside world, the more thou will have to clear later.

What goes in comes out, and what comes out goes in. The universe desires growth for thee, but it cannot help you if thou art clinging to the things that keep thee small. Thee shall, therefore, experience constant resistance until thou surrender, because the universe, or God (whichever you prefer) is infinitely relentless.

What happens if one does not let go in the face of resistance is the same thing that happened to the titanic when the captain did not see the iceberg as a threat. Know that anything keeping thee small is a giant threat to not only thy thrival, but thy survival. For if thou will not step into thy dharma, the universe will end the game so thou can start over. The universe is not going to waste thy time.

Like a child, the universe cannot stand to be

bored; for it only lives in the present moment. By keeping the universe entertained through constantly evolving, changing, growing, learning and creating one keeps the universe's favor. That is where luck comes from. It is said that luck is what happens when hard work meets opportunity. Actually, luck is what happens when heart work meets opportunity. The universe doesn't want to watch thee work hard, that's boring, the universe wants to see you having an incredible fucking time with the gifts it gave thee. The universe will only watch you work hard for a short time until it gets bored and thou notice doors stop opening for thee as much.

It is written, "be childlike", because the universe is as a child, and thou art reflection of the universe. Follow thy nature. Beings from other dimensions come here to try and take humans out of their true nature, which is play, creation, healing, and love. Those beings have enslaved mankind, pinning us against one-another, leading humans to believe life is serious. Life isn't serious, life is a joke… that's why the Buddha is always laughing.

If thou refuseth change, the universe directs energy elsewhere. Towards openness. That is why there is so much creation in existence, look at all there is. Like a child, the universe has zero judgement, everything just is what it is. A person never judged a thing until the illusive concepts of right and wrong were drilled into their mind.

Most people feel being alone is unbearable, but most people never really get the chance to be in complete solitude for extended periods of time. Solitude is a luxury. If thou hast the opportunity to be alone, you are lucky. Some people in the world are so surrounded by people, they do not have the option to be alone.

One must be alone before they can truly know them self. To find the purpose, one must first learn to be comfortable with being alone. To find peace in solitude is a worthy purpose for most.

Humans are meant to connect and live in community; this is how they evolved to survive. The challenge is, the addiction to connection and comfort makes it difficult for people to break free and spend time with others out of will rather than need. It is only alone that people truly find themselves.

A major part of finding the self is the discovery of one's gifts, inspirations and passions—their ideas.

Alone is where God speaks the loudest. This is another reason most people cannot bear to be alone; they don't want to face their shadow. In facing one's shadow they are met with two options, to either endure an ego death and grow, or to continue down the same path and whither.

Meditation helps with building the comfort of solitude. While alone, one may sharpen their craft, so they can bring great gifts into the world that will better the lives of as many beings as possible.

Public speaking is only most people's greatest fear because most people are overly concerned with what others think of them. The anxiety that surrounds what others think of them comes from the need to be accepted, which stems from the discomfort with being alone.

Once people become comfortable with solitude, they no longer fear rejection. Then they can truly be their self, and rejection ceases to become a part of their reality. The fear of public speaking fades away, allowing their spiritual gifts to shine through.

The cure for the fear of public speaking is not just to practice public speaking, it is to be alone until worth is no longer dependent on the acceptance of others. One may push their own boundary until they are comfortable with solitude. The moment thou releaseth all need to be needed, everyone needs thee. Then thou wish everyone would just leave you alone. So, the grass is always greener, thee might as well just enjoy life where thou art, and let it take thee on a beyoutiful journey.

Unity consciousness, God consciousness, enlightenment, or whatever one chooses to call it, is discovered in solitude. Everything is discovered where there is nothing, for everything comes from the void. Light is particular matter, and matter is something. If God said let there be light, then God spoke from the darkness which means that before there was light God was the ruler over darkness. So do not fear darkness, for even God lives there.

Some monks have 40-day dark room meditations with non-human contact, which releases natural amounts of DMT and induces Godly experiences.

One may find God in the darkness, not only in the light. Rejoice in all things. The light lives in the darkness, thou just have to open thy eye.

Enlightening is a constant process, but there is no enlightened, for there is no destination. There is only in-light-in-meant, meaning thou art meant for the light. And it's a process.

One has already arrived; enlightenment is simply a matter of awakening where thou art. You are already here, so the more here you can be the more enlightened you are. It takes more strength to surrender than it does to control. For every new arrival there is a new destination. Every moment is a no arrival, so flow within the moments between the seconds, that is where God lives.

Wherever ye go there art thou. There is no finish line, even the present moment exists on an infinite spectrum of depth. The depth of the present moment is eternal. With every door one opens, ten more doors open. One should enjoy the process, and by tapping into joy they are enlightening. Also, by allowing one's self to sink into depression, they are also enlightening. Depression is the first stage of enlightenment.

To be enlightened, is to be enlightening. Enlightenment is the process of letting go of that which is not serving thy highest light. Where thou art is perfect, for this is where God, the universe, yoniverse, creator, Santa Clause, higher power, or whatever, has placed thee.

51

The earthly realm is here to allow people to rise into a state of love for all that exists seemingly outside of them. The rise is a joyous process. To exist is to exit, to insist is to remain.

The attachment to things that exist is overly focused on the outside world. Thus, causing thee to exit the present moment. The outside world is a distraction from what lives inside, for those who have not yet found peace within their heart. In that way it is true, "Be in the world, but not of the world." The outside world is not just coming in, it is going out, the observer is creating it.

The desire to become enlightened is a trick that causes people to avoid the present moment, instead of approach it.

One who forgets about enlightenment, begins to enlighten naturally, for there is no longer attachment to the goal of enlightenment. The desire to enlighten stems from the lack of acceptance for what is, but enlightenment is the result of accepting what is. Enlightenment is the result of acceptance.

Enlightenment is a biproduct of love. The more you love the more ye let go of. You let go of thy judgments, shame, anger, need, and all the other things pulling down on thee. Love lightens the load. The more one loves the faster they ascend. You can't love everyone for them, ye can only love everyone for thee. For they truly are thee, but by focusing on them thou may focus away from thy journey which is truly all ye have.

If ye aren't loving thy self-first then ye don't have any love to give them, in which case what ye think ye are giving them isn't love. Make loving thyself thou primary objective, and let all other objectives naturally rise in line after that. In opening one's self to oneness, one becomes sacred. It is the sacred who ascend.

Love is courageous. Love is the hardest decision to make, but the easiest thing you could ever do. Love is the superior act of surrender.

As long as you are living, you are learning. Life is about learning, not knowing. True masters have not mastered the state of knowing, they have mastered the state of learning. Zen masters learn about themselves in all circumstances. Humility is the willingness to learn. Humility is the wisest of all states for reality is perception. The reality that is perceived by the receiver is scripted by the transmitter before it can become a reality. By remaining conscious and aware of one's thoughts at all times, one may consciously manifest the reality they were born to inspire.

There is no reality other than what is perceived. One's perceived reality is real to them, and if they act on that reality, they make it real to the world too. By choosing positive, loving realities, one makes the world a better place for all possible of all dimensions. There is a butterfly effect. Realize ye, how powerful thou art. One person shifted with thy love, shifts two people with that same vibration, who shift 4 people, who shift 8 people, who shift 16 people. Life is a cascade, the Fibonacci sequence. Thou art powerful beyond measure and ye change the world with every breath ye take. Breathe love and watch thine dream become more beautiful.

Reality isn't a thing until it becomes a story. Reality is the story one tells that become the things they call reality, real eye tea. Ye drinketh what thou seest, and then what thou seeth thou drinkest. Every being has a different perception of reality.

No two people live in the same world. Choose people who see thy greatest version of self in thee. What ye see in others, ye put in them, and what ye put in others, ye pull out of them.

The less ye love thyself, the greater thy temper will be. The more one loves their self, the more easily they make peace. Love doesn't want war, only hatred wants war. Love wants peace, so you know what a person is made of depending on what they seek to inspire in the world.

A person's temper is their weakest link. Love is an umbrella. Love cannot be defined; love is the purpose of everything.

The human race has been programmed to fear love, so that they would be cut off from their purpose, and thus easier to control. It is impossible to control a person who is love for they move at the beat of their own heart, that beat which harmonizes with the entire universe.

Humankind was tricked into thinking that lust is love, so that even if they learn to place love first, they would be led astray. Lust is fine in its own right and deserves liberation like all things, but it has nothing to do with love.

All mankind really wants is peace, yet the world has people fighting each other for it. How much sense does it make to fight for peace? Fighting for peace is like stealing from those who steal in the name of justice. One may only find people by being peace, for as long as they think it's okay to fight the fight will continue. For it is the consciousness that needs to evolve before the world can follow.

Fighting does not cause peace. Fighting causes pain, and pain causes more fighting. Peace starts where blaming ends.

6 MONEY

Dreams are the substance life is made
from.

One does not work for money, they work for a purpose, and let money work for them.

Money is infinite. All the money one could ever need is already all around them. Manifesting money is a matter of trading what one currently has, for what they believe it is worth. One deserves what they believe they are worth. Thine worth, is whatever ye say it is. Nobody chooses ye worth other than thee. If one believes it, so will others and believing it so makes it so.

One must always under promise and over deliver if they want longevity in success. A person may attract as much money as they can see and comprehend. This is why the rich tend to stay rich, not just because of privilege, no but that is what they want ye to think. It is easier to manifest what one has already seen. In order to earn change in exchange for something, one must make something that causes a positive change in the way people function.

Business isn't about making money, business is about making the world a better place. This is why art is so crucial. A person can turn anything into a work of art. They can even turn math into art. A true artist is always successful. One should make their craft an art, so that it can be unique and individual to their self. That will greatly increase the value of their service.

Eighty-five percent of people try to emanate what successful people have already done. 10% of people don't try to be successful at all. And 5% of people walk to the beat of their own drum. Those 85% don't realize that what those 5% did was follow their heart.

Repeat this in thy mind for 31 minutes. When thou art one with the sun thou art one with the son, then ye work becomes play and ye life becomes fun. Christ consciousness is service to the one.

When thou art one with the sun thou art one with the son, then ye work becomes play and ye life becomes fun.

Everything is a product of something. Everything is either a medicine, or a poison. Either poison or medicine can be sold for the same amount. So ye might as well make things that heal people, rather than things that make them sick.

If you add true value to people's lives, you become a more valuable person. Value is assessed by the impact one has on other people, but worth is subjective. Money is not an exchange of worth, but of value. One is worth whatever they believe they are worth, but their value is based on perception. Value is an exchange for time, energy and spiritual gifts. If one wants to make more money, they can trade more time, energy, and market their spiritual gifts.

Those who waste their time, energy and spiritual gifts, do not love life because those are the three things life is made of. One's worth is proportional to their value, because people market their spiritual gifts to the extent that they believe their own worth. If ye believe thou art worthy, ye will heavily market thine gifts; knowing that others need them and are willing to pay a valuable price.

Only you can make thy dreams come true, but others must support thee in doing so. So you must also support others, for as above so below. Dreams are the substance life is made from. Those who do not have a dream, will not meet their potential in the amount of money they will attract. Money is not the meaning of life, obviously, but having money helps people to live better lives. So those who truly love life, also love money, knowing that they support one another.

Those who judge only put walls around themselves. Those who judge money block themselves from receiving all forms of abundance.

Sales is not just a business strategy or department within a company, sales is a natural part of life. However, most people judge the process of sales, which is why it makes them uncomfortable. People do not like the idea of selling something because they feel it places them below someone else, but if only they humble them self shall they be exalted.

Beggars can't be choosers, but sellers can.

From my perspective, there are only three types of salespeople; The Beggar, The Shark, and The Maverick.

The Beggar is someone who does not actually believe their own worth but tries to guilt people into meeting their own self-proclaimed value.

The Shark is someone who also does not actually believe their own worth and tries to manipulate others in meeting their own self-proclaimed value.

The Maverick is a person who does believe their own worth, and therefore guides others into their own self-proclaimed value through delivery, rather than show. The Maverick always under promises and over delivers because these types of salesperson sees others as equal to themselves, neither above nor below, but one in the same. The Maverick naturally treats others as they would have others treat them, and that is why sales for The Maverick does not feel like selling anything, but rather sharing of one's spiritual gifts in exchange for a mutually agreed upon value.

Sales is a form of leadership, the process of recruiting other people to thy perspective. Practice the mastery of non-response. One who does not respond holds space for others to think. While thinking, people are eventually confronted by themselves. While selling a concept, idea, or thing, do not interrupt the buyer's thought process for once confronted by themselves they are able to tell thee what they need in order to be comfortable with making the purchase.

The reason that beggars and sharks do not hold space for others to think, is that they are afraid others will not honor their value. This is due to the fact that beggars and sharks do not honor their own value, as they do not actually believe their worth.

Inspire people to think, so that they may show thee their thoughts. While observing their thoughts ask them what they want. In order to share thy gift with the world, ye must be willing to sell thy gift to the world. If one does not receive compensation for their gifts, they will not be able to make more. It's not greedy to require compensation, it is classy.

Worth is the key to class. What separates those who have class from those who do not is self-worth. Money, friends, fame, power and nothing else can give a person class. Only the beliefs that one holds for themself will determine whether or not they are classy. If one believes he is a King, then he will hold themselves like a king, even if he has no possessions. If others do not believe he is a king they cannot see the royalty alive within them self. If one does not believe he is a king he will constantly try to prove his worth to not only others, but to himself, and then no matter what he has, he will not have class. Class is knowing thy worth. Those with class do not seek external validation, and because they do not seek it they attract it.

There is no partnership other than the partnership

with thy self. People think they have partners, but truly those partners are simply manifestations of their belief systems. If one is not happy with their partner they may leave the relationship, or they may change them self. But to stay in an unhappy relationship is self-sabotage, a reflection of one's own self determined lack of worth.

Forgiveness is not only the way to heal others, forgiveness is the way to illuminate thyself. Forgiveness is freedom from thine cave. Forgiveness is release from thy cage.

For we came here to heal each other, not to scorn one another. A woman only doubts her self-worth because her father did not confirm to her that she was a queen before the age of 6, and a man only doubts his self-worth because his mother did not confirm to him that he is a king before the age of 6. People have a window to empower their babies called the critical years of development which is from 1-6 years young. After 6, it becomes difficult to rewire the pattern. A healed woman has the responsibility to treat men like their mothers never did and a healed man has the responsibility to treat women like their fathers never did.

Money is never a problem for someone who does not have self-worth issues. Once a person heals their self-worth issues, their money problems fade, and the fastest and most direct method of healing self worth issues is through their relationship with the opposite sex.

This does not mean that everyone with money is healed of self-worth issues, because some people do corrupt and destructive things to make money, that only perpetuates their wounds. It is said that it is easier to fit a camel through the eye of a needle than for a rich person to enter the kingdom of heaven. In order to make money in a way that makes the world a better place, and people healthier, one must have already healed their wounds with the opposite sex.

Wounds are blessings because in the process of healing, one ignites a momentum that catapults their spiritual gifts and explodes their success. It is becoming easier and easier to fit camels through the eyes of needles in today's world. We see camels walking through needles all the time now.

Those who judge will sales will not attract money, and those who judge in general will struggle to give their gifts to the world while respecting their own worth. If one does not respect their worth, they quickly run out of time and energy.

Money is here to compensate people for their incredibly valuable time and energy, so that they can continue to be fed while serving. One who can see how beautiful money is, will not struggle to attract money. For beauty is the magic of attraction. That is the law of attraction at work. If ye desire, meditate on how beautiful is thy desire and it will come forth. But one who desires often resents, despises or hates what they do not have, pushing it away. It sounds like common sense, but it is not common to think this way.

What one loves, they attract. One who loves life, loves experience, for life is experience. Love money, if you want to open the possibilities for more life experience. Those who love money attract money with ease and grace. Love everything if ye want abundance.

To learn is to expand, to forget is to contract. As people give, they remember and experience peace. As people take, they forget and experience temporary moments of spiritual amnesia. By taking people actually lose, not gain.

Bit by bit, they sell their soul. They sell their soul to the void in exchange for validation. As the void grows, it will never be enough. The more people have, the more they want. Utilize thy money to give.

Everything people take is done in an attempt to fill the void. The more people put in the void the bigger the void grows. When the taker begins to give, then they begin to live, and the void diminishes.

Giving is living. While acquiring money, those who do that which they do not love end up resenting money, as they blame money for their own decision to sell bits of their soul. But money never does anything, people do things. Money doesn't make decisions, people make them. Money never did anything for thee, you did things for money. You can either do things you love for money or do things you hate for money. Transforming from one who works for money to one who has money work for them is as swift as a simple switch of the switch.

Media causes some people to forget who they are, which is to forget their spiritual gifts. Media is a collective ego. Media comes from Medea, the Goddess of Illusion.

One's hobby can be their trade for money, and one's passion can be their hobby. To serve the self is to care for the Ego. If ye do not care for thy ego, the collective ego will take over thy vessel. It is important to love thyself first, because the concept of self is an ego construct, so if thou do not feed thine ego it will weaken and not have the strength to overpower the collective ego, which is in constant battle for thy soul.

Thy vessel is the container of thine energy. The collective ego is a giant being who has taken over countless bodies by convincing them that they are not giants. Always remember thou art a giant. The collective ego leads people forgetting that they are giants by convincing them that they are more of a giant than others, that is a lie. You are no more of a giant than anyone else, for we are all giants. Lies the collective ego feeds people feels stimulating, but the truth is relaxing. People become addicted to stimulation, but they could just as easily become addicted to relaxation. Whatever thou art fed will become thy pattern, so feed ye thy dreams. Do not let others feed ye their dreams.

To care for the higher self is to serve others. To serve the ego before the soul is to miss the mark, for the self is so much greater than the confines of the human body. To serve the ego before the soul is to engage in sin, which depletes the soul of its light.

It is often through fasting that one comes to realize their true fullness. It is often through purposeful restriction that one comes to realize their true wholeness.

It is often through fasting that one comes to realize their true fullness. It is often through purposeful restriction that one comes to realize their true wholeness. This is why profits throughout history have practiced voluntary fasting and restriction for 40+ days at a time. Ormus helps with both fasting and restriction as it nourishes the vessel with light, easing the process. Sun gazing at sunrise and at sunset also helps with fasting and restriction as the sun is a form of food for the soul.

The sun is spelled as sol in languages and pronounced as soul, and hearty meals are called soul food because ancients have always known that the sun feeds our soul with light codes needed for our evolution.

No matter the disease, nature has the remedy. Those who listen for as long as it takes to hear the heart, become one with nature. For when the heartbeat of ye is one with the heartbeat of earth thy body will turn from a state of disease into a state of ease. The heart is the source of one's intuition, not what people think of as the brain. In actuality the brain is the totality of the entire body, as it all works together.

Sometimes, one must take an intermission (inner mission) from the world outside and go within, in order to find their purpose. Society will tell ye that thou art insane if thy life leaves them to meet thyself, but only because misery loves company. If people tell thee that thou art going insane it may be because you are moving into sanity. To go in-sane, is the first step in realizing that they are crazy and realizing that they are crazy is the first step of awakening out of craziness into lucid living wakefulness.

Do not fear craziness, for in order to awaken one must step into their own craziness to illuminate the darkness that resides within them. For craziness is only a lack of awareness. The process of awakening always requires solitude and can begin as seemingly unbearable. We came from the womb into a crazy world and must move through another womb into sanity while we still exist in this realm, which is as Jesus would say, to be born again.

One should never check out of themselves to check in to a job. By doing things out of alignment with purpose, just to make money, people chip away at pieces of their heart. If a person does that which they do not intrinsically love, just to make money, they will eventually no longer love themself.

Once a person no longer loves themself, they will no longer be capable of loving anything, including life. Always do what you would do if money did not exist. Live for impacting the world and you will never need to worry about having money again, for thou shall grow richer and richer every day. For eternal fulfillment, or what people call "happy", do what you would do if money did not exist. A person who cannot be purchased is unstoppable in their endeavors.

Go into nature and listen for as long as it takes, until all of life becomes an inner mission. A person's method of art is their spiritual gift. One's art is the key to their heart, and one's heart is path to their destiny on plan it Earth, where we all planned our darma before we arrived here, to hear our calling, which is our destiny. So only through the heart space may we hear our destiny.

Art is not just painting, dancing, music, and so on. Any activity one puts their heart into, becomes an art form expression of their deep seeded darma.

The voice of the heart is not soft. The heart is like a jaguar; strong, courageous, powerful, unstoppable, and piercing right through the darkness. The Jaguar is called Jaguar, because it pierces through the vail allowing a sliver of light to shine through into the unknown, and all that is required to illuminate an entire realm is just a sliver of light. For where that sliver of light came from is an abundance of light great enough to dissolve the entire vail veil of darkness.

What the heart commands one to do will not serve just their ego, for the ego contains a fight-or-flight mechanism healed within the spine and leading up to the amygdala. The ego triggers people to fight against or to run from anything that does not serve the body, pleasure, stimulation, immediate gratification and comfort. Heald within the spine is also the kundalini, but that is the light of the spine and leads up to the pineal gland.

What the heart commands one to do will serve their kundalini, which feels physically similar to ego, but more ecstatically blissful, less stimulating, and illuminates thy soul.

One may believe they have reached enlightenment, but enlightenment is nothing to obtain, so if they believe they have reached enlightenment they are even further from enlightenment then before they ever knew what enlightenment was.

7 WISDOM

Anxiety is the universe tapping you on
the shoulder, telling you something in
your life needs to change.

God is non-dualistic. The ego feeds on being
right. One may find more ego in those who are
righteous, than anywhere else. The ego literally lives
to be right; it is impossible for the ego to be wrong.
To accept that one does not know is an ego death
upon itself.

One who knows does not know, and one who
does not know, knows.

Be aware of the quiet ones, for the quiet ones
know everything. Beware of the chatty ones, for the
chatty ones know nothing. A quiet one may disguise
themselves as a chatty one simply to hide the fact
that they know everything. A chatty one may hide
themselves as a quiet one to disguise the fact that
they know nothing. So beware of both, but as
always, fear nothing. The more ye understandeth, the
less that frightens thee.

In times of nervousness, the warrior embodies
their truth vibrationally before saying a word. When
a warrior stands in their truth, one may knowtice that

nothing needs to be said. Truth will be felt and the effects of feeling are stronger than the effects of talking.

People who live to please, satisfy – or in any other way receive validation have not yet found the sound of their own heart. Ye must hear thine heart if thou art to awaken thy destiny. Worship thy fear no longer. Meditate.

A man with nothing owns everything. A woman who has given everything away has gained it all. People may appear peaceful while everything is going their way, but if life took away their job, car, social status, relationship, or whatever else they think is bringing them validation in the form of external approval, they would lose their minds. Validation is how people who have not yet found themselves ID themselves through the opinions of others. To become truly rich, one first must let go of their need for validation.

Some people lose their minds when they lose their possessions because the idea of possessing anything is of the mind. Some people are possessed by their possessions because they rely on things outside of themselves to give them a sense of self, an identity.

To them, losing their things is losing their identity, which is an ego death, because ego in and of itself is the expression of the identification construct. So those people would fight for their lives to protect their possessions, because to their ego their entire life is their idea of self. The ego does not know that self can change, without the person dying, because the personality is the ego. If the personality changes, the ego dies and a new ego takes form. The antidote to war is overcoming the fear of death, which naturally leads to listening.

A heavy heart is brought to peace upon knowing that what is not meant for it will pass it by, and what is meant for it will stay.

The present moment is God's gift. One who knows they deserve the gift of presence, allows their self to be still, and know that "I am God". Only in stillness do they receive the present moment, and one who has first mastered stillness may take stillness into extreme movement and become highly effective unto the world around them.

It's not but first coffee, it's but first stillness. One who has found the present moment has a Godly presence about them, one who has found coffee has more ego…

While one may feel like they are in a mess, they are actually being blessed. Leaps and bounds can be messy. With patience, one may be able to see, once the dust has settled, that all of the destruction was actually construction.

One may go far by moving slow. Opportunity can be ruined by not thoroughly thinking things through. Sometimes, one must move fast, or they will miss the opportunity by not giving it enough gusto.

Wisdom is having the foresight to know when to

move fast and when to move slow. Wisdom is also knowing how to apply foresight.

When movement arises from stillness, it is inspired by spirit. One who seeks wisdom, finds all other things they could possibly want.

Wisdom is the one thing that never goes and always grows. Wisdom is the only thing that will always build upon itself. Wisdom is the only true investment. One may have a lot of money and with it destroy their life. Destroy their health, family and happiness. Then they could lose their money too and be worse off than they were before the money came. But when one invests in wisdom, all dynamics of life grow with it, even love, fore wisdom begets wisdom.

One with an empty cup can neither drink for them self, nor can they pour for others. Wisdom is knowing when to pour and when to fill.

One who's greatest loyalty is to wisdom can always be full to support others. Service is how one expresses their unique spiritual gifts to the world. Everything comes together naturally when one is loyal to their service, because thy service is the only thing, thou art meant to control. One cannot control others, and the desire to do so would drain them.

We can guide, but never control. If others want to make a mistake, and will not trust our guidance, we should let them make their mistakes and then come to trust our guidance. Will they be hurt? Yes, but rather let someone hurt themselves than let them hurt thee, for if thou let them hurt you, they will only continue to hurt others until eventually they hurt themselves too.

The mind and body are one, so psychological health and physical health have a direct relationship with one another, compounding upon each other. As one cares for their psychology it becomes instinctual to care for their body, and as one cares for their body, spiritual practice (such as healthy eating and spending time with positive people) becomes instinctual also.

Physical health involves sleep, positive thoughts, moderate yet consistent exercise, and intuitive (int-you-it-eye-ive) nutrition.

Spiritual health involves nature, time alone, decisiveness with who one spends their time with, spiritual play, and service.

The relationship with self is the primary relationship of all. If one neglects any one of these components, they will find that the other components begin to suffer. Wisdom leads to balance.

People often think they are separate from God. But a person is that which they pray to, and that which prays to them. Giving to another is to realize one's true nature, which is abundance.

Taking from another is taking from thyself. By giving to another, one gives to thyself. Therefore, sometimes giving to another is the ultimate act of self-love. By taking from another, one makes them self poor. Some millionaires and billionaires in the world are poor.

Even with all their money they feel small and need to put others down to experience a sense of power. However, if one becomes a billionaire by giving, then they are truly rich. Easier to fit through the eye of a needle... but that doesn't make it impossible. As it is written, so it shall be done. One who writes their intents experiences them. The universe is a Genie's lamp. Thy voice is a wizard's wand. Magic is conscious languaging. Abracadabra means I create as I speak. Every word thee speaketh is a spell unto thy new realities. Some people think it's okay to vent negatively, unaware of their own power as a creator.

We hear people tell negative stories about themselves and others, without knowing that they are actually cursing their own life, and the lives of others (there is no difference). Thy life, and everything ye speak is a song. Ye days are numbered, each day a page of thy song.

Make thou song a positive, beautiful, and uplifting one. Do not sing dark, negative, destructive songs, or else ye shalt experience a painful life. Sing a light, loving song that ye shalt experience a beautiful life. When others sing their negative song, do not be a people pleaser and agree with what they say, otherwise thou allow them to recruit thee into their nightmare. Life is thy dream.

All people want to be celebrated; to be received is to be celebrated. All people want to feel worthy; to be blessed with the gift of presence. Thy undivided attention is the greatest gift thee could ever give. All people hold all of these feelings within them already. In school they do not teach the golden rule, they teach a curriculum that is destined to be forgotten, for it is not applicable to life.

Patience is the key to peace, and peace unlocks patience. Patience and peace work together to support one another. All things co-exist. All things are a symbol of infinity. Without that which is not there can be no that which is. Power is the ability to control, which is why with great power comes great responsibility. Power brings choice. The behavior of wisdom is seeking knowledge, for knowledge is the doorway to power, and power is the source of all creation. Everything begins at the one defining moment when thy awareness, which is love, makes the decision to speak something into existence with the voice that is the presence of power.

Sometimes people withhold their truth for fear of judgment and ridicule. One must be vulnerable enough to risk being ostracized in order to speak their truth. To speak one's truth is to expose their heart, and risk rejection, but rejection is not real. One who shames those who have the courage to speak their truth lose their own power and begin to fear speaking their own truth. This is the mechanism of karma in action.

One must be courageous to speak their truth. Creation is an act of courage. God is courageous, are we not created in God's image? Courage should always be rewarded, in fact, courage is always reworded. Reword the script to thy life by leveling up the lyrics.

As one practices speaking consciously, they become more confident, and speaking their truth becomes more natural over time as they begin to see positive results. Their power grows in response to speaking their truth. Everything is a cascade.

Sometimes begging for what one believes in is strength. Sometimes asking for help is humble. No hand can scratch itself. If the other hand is full, ask for help. It's not always easy to ask for help; this is why the humble are exalted. In this we, one who allows their self to beg may go far and create empires.

Beggars actually can be choosers, when they know what they need, and settle for nothing less. If ye beggeth for fish do not accept bread, else thee find thyself begging for fish again tomorrow and thy life becometh purgatory. If it is fish, thou needest, wait for fish. If ye beggeth for fish but accept bread, the next day thou art twice as likely to receive bread. Everything is a cascade.

Before asking for help, one must admit that they cannot do it alone, which is another form of ego death. The ego wants to do everything alone. A self-made person has not made very much at all. One can pick themselves up and become stronger by doing so. But, no one can build an empire alone, unless it is an empire of loneliness.

Rome was not built in a day, but the Earth was. Do not think that building an empire must take a lifetime. It can happen tomorrow. Be open to all possibilities (possabilities). Continue to shine thy gifts until they are so reflective that they project magic into the world. Rome may not have been built in a day, but all of mankind was. God simply said, "let there be light", and there was light. God said, "let there be man" and there was man. Believe that God can also say, "Let there be... fill in the blank". Mankind was created in the image of God, to speak its truth into existence, knowing that everything it speaks becomes reality (real-it-eye). Be aware of thy thoughts for they are the evidence of thy beliefs. Be aware of thy beliefs for they become thy words and be aware of thy words for they are the magic spells that shape the codes of thine matrix. Just as the assembly of letters into words is called spelling, let it be said, and so it is.

As children, people were sometimes punished in response to asking for help. When children requested help from an adult who did not have the ability to help them, those adults may have become frustrated at their self-imposed lack of ability. Even though these adults were frustrated with themselves, they took it out on the children. By forgiving all beings who have ever hurt one, they may free them self up to ask for help again.

By asking for help in a reverent manner, not with expectations or attachment, one receives with grace and ease. Remember that if it is truly needed, it will come. Ask with an openness to receive any response that God has in store for thee, knowing this response is the universe's blessing. The universe, youinverse, or whatever one chooses to call it, knows what they need in order to accomplish the mission they were destined to achieve.

If the universe can turn a caterpillar into a butterfly without any help from the caterpillar whatsoever, even without the caterpillar knowing what is happening, imagine what the universe can do for thee. Remember, thou art no greater than a caterpillar and a caterpillar is no greater than thee. One who intentionally and carelessly steps on an ant, puts out into the uni-verse that it is ok to be carelessly, and intentionally stepped on. By intentionally destroying another one would intentionally destroy them self.

All the caterpillar needs to do in order to become its butterfly counterpart is consume as much food as possible, and the caterpillar loves eating. And so, it is, that all ye must do in order to become thy greatest version of self is what you love the most. So, isn't life beautiful?

Sometimes what people think they need would only be a distraction from what is actually good for them. When the universe pusheth anything out of thy life, let it go; like a butterfly.

Where help cannot be found, by continuing to work as heart as possible and remaining focused on the mission, one eventually attracts the tribe that was waiting for them to be ready for it. Everybody is calling everything in. What ye needest, needeth thee.

The team is already here, waiting for thy vibration to align with it. Keep loving on thyself, to raise thine vibration until thou art blown away and amazed in awe of all thine reflections that surround thee. Thy vibration builds thine nation. In order to assemble a team of supportive mates, one must continue to raise their frequency, by letting go of that which does not serve them (them being their highest calling-not their ego).

Always Meditation before medication. Some people take drugs to achieve emotional and psychiatric relief. Tension is the universe trying to turn ye into thy greatest version, like the diamond. By seeking relief, one would only interrupt the process. The caterpillar builds its own cocoon and lets itself literally melt away in extreme discomfort. The feeling is somewhat similar to eating a hand full of mushrooms, I'd imagine, but it's always better to reach these states without substances for only when thy seed blossoms naturally does it blossom permanently.

People are so avoidant of depression and discomfort that they avoid leaving their own evolution. Many times, that anxiety and depression is just an issue lingering in the dark abyss of the subconscious waiting to be discovered, faced and loved.

Anxiety is the universe tapping you on the shoulder, letting you know that something in your life needs to change.

Through meditation one discovers their deeper issues, and only by dis-covering these issues may one change them. An addiction is a behavior that puts more layers over one's issues, burying them with distance rather than dis-covering. So naturally, problems arise from that void. Problems are the worlds feedback. Those problems attempt to show addicts that they have something to face.

With that distance their issues have room to grow. The issues crave the addicted behavior, because in the presence of the addicted behavior the issue can live itself out through the subject, like a host. Know that an addictive behavior is an entity; it can be starved, extracted or transmuted with love. The addiction is not the issue, the addiction is the result of the issue gone unnoticed for long periods of time. To stop the addiction, find the issue, do not mask it.

The distance created by addictive behaviors allow the void to continuously grow, constantly expanding, and becoming the separation from self. It is this void that people try to fill with drugs, relationships and things. However, as people fill the void, it grows even bigger.

The void cannot be filled, it must be healed. Only through healing will the void close itself. Love is the medicine. Wisdom is the wizard's wand of love.

Issues are wounds crying out to be loved, not ignored, abandoned, judged, condemned, shamed, neglected, or in any other way feared. Before going on medication, try meditation. Meditation is the greatest act of self-love. Meditate at 4:44am, for 44 minutes each day, for 44 days. Always set a positive affirmation prior to meditation in order to guide a more conscious experience. The use of Ormus can activate the affirmation and catalyze the meditation. Ormus is the essential nutrient above anything else. Nothing can be without it.

One might observe the word intentions, and question whether having intentions put them in tension. The word intention has tension pronounced into it. Indeed, one's intentions may interrupt the natural state of being, which is to play, and to be present for what the universe has predestined. If one goes into a moment with a specific intention they may be attached to that outcome. When things are done in a playful manner, what is meant to be happens naturally. Children are always in awe of life's magic unfolding around them. Children let the universe be a magician because they do not try to control everything. This why children are held at the highest seating and revered as magicians in ancient occult, paganistic philosophies; including The Bible.

To have an intention might mean that one is not already enough. An affirmation is an I am statement; an intention is a goal. There is no other mind than the goal-oriented mind. To be purposeful is to have a destination. Meditate with a purpose and an affirmation. Always have a purpose but remain open to what the universe knows is best for all.

One must remain aware of the words within the

words they choose, if they are to awaken within the dream that is life.

Many don't believe they have time to meditate, yet they have time to do all the things that cause them to have a need to meditate. The truth is that people don't have time not to meditate. Life is too short and moves too fast to not sit back in the seat of thy soul. One can only say they have time to do things that cause them anxiety, but don't have time to do things that alleviate it for one reason; the lack of self-love.

8 LOVE

Love is the force that holds all things
together.

Failure is not the evidence of weakness; failure is the evidence of strength. Failure is the beginning of growth. In the gym failure is celebrated and strived for, but in life sometimes people forget that failure is a target to obtain, for without reaching failure one could never push their limits.

One's relationship with others can only be as healthy as is their relationship to self. Society has romanticized the state called being "in love." True love has nothing to do with romance or sex. But there are 5 types of love and if one is to move into any type of love, without patiently establishing the first love, it will not last. And when it leaves will have taken their time and energy. Eye have learned that love without discernment is dangerous. Love occurs in stages and must follow the following format in order to be infinitely successful:

The first love is unconditional. This is the love one should have for thyself, and for all things extending from thyself, which is all things. Unconditional love is understanding; the act of wisdom.

The second love is philautia, the love that one has for their self, family, and friends. One may establish philautia without ever moving through eros and philia, but not without unconditional love. Philautia deals mainly with the self, for if one cannot know thyself, then they cannot know anyone else. One must awaken through unconditional love before they can come to know them self.

Philia is the affectionate love, and often times becomes sexual because it contains within it a component of energetic magnetism. Philia, like eros, can become addicting because it feels so good to the senses. To step into philia before establishing unconditional love can result in frustration and anger, as well as heart break. Philia before eros can result in STDs, Sexually Transmitted Demons.

The fourth love is Eros. Eros is romantic love, and often becomes sexual or lustful. Some people move into eros love before unconditional love is established. That is the Disney programming at work. Eros love before agape is the beginning of delusion. Eros often involves commitment, in healthy cases. To step into eros without first establishing unconditional love can result in disastrous scars to the pain body, for eros is a fire energy, and fire burns things.

Pragma love is a love who has endured over time through many challenges. The pain resulted in wisdom. Those with pragma love for one another first established unconditional love, have moved through all other stages, and often times have created a family together and will endure eternally as one unit, lifetime after lifetime.

The love society speaks of is mostly eros, philia and philautia, but very rarely unconditional and pragma. This is because eros, philia and philautia can result in immediate gratification and the ego loves immediate gratification.

Discernment before love is self-love. Tie ye not to something that is not good for thee, less thou be required to learn unfortunate lessons in-order to sever the bonds.

Love unlocks the heart. Hand the key over to only those with sacred reverence, otherwise they would throw a party in the heart and leave when there is nothing left to get drunk on.

Because love awakens all of the spirits within the temple, it opens the door for more lessons than anything else. To choose discernment before love is self-love. One who loves others before them self, ends up with only less to give.

One loves them self by giving energy and time to things and people that graciously humble them, but not that drain them. Humility worships those in service to the God.

A wise person intends on attracting people who humble them, not who boost their ego. If someone tells them everything they want to hear, they don't truly love them, nor do they truly love themselves.

Love those who are gracefully real with you in the spirit of expansion.

Spiritual bypass is the act of feeding the ego in the name of spirituality. Ego is clever in that way, it befriends its enemies, like a colorful snake. It wants to be likeable, so they will let it in. Ego knows how to catch bees. Ego lives most, where it is most threatened, and it hides there. Ego, like the military, has spies in all enemy territory.

Service to the world is one of the three gateways to happiness. We arrived here to leave things even more beautiful than before we came.

Love is the warrior's path; it takes courage to practice that discernment, and strength to follow through with it. Love is not meant to be easy at first. Love makes people stronger. Love is designed this way because strength is required for growth. As a feeling, surrendering into a state of love is bliss, of course, but if not done with discernment then the higher people go the harder, they fall.

Have faith, but do not have blind faith. Only sheep have blind faith, which is actually hope. Those who tell stories about failed relationships, making one person out to be a perpetrator, and the other out to be the victim, forget the truth of discernment.

All experience leads to knowledge, and all knowledge is self-knowledge, so everything happens for you.

It is said that the true meaning of sin is to miss the mark. To sin is a mistake. Just step back and take another look. Recalibrate, re-aim and release. We are all archers.

Each new day begins with a rising, not a mourning. To say good rising instead of good morning is a way to start the day off on a positive trajectory instead of a negative one. The word morning comes from the word, to mourn, which has a negative connotation to it, and implies the loss of something. A better way to start the day, is with a rising. Each rising is a new birthday, a new beginning, and an ascension. Get up and rise, don't get up and mourn.

Perhaps mourning comes from the mourning of all the mistakes from the previous day, but one learns from all mistakes which they are willing to take responsibility for, and they rise from them, like a phoenix through the fires of karma.

Each new morning is a rising, and a mistake is a lesson, which is a blessing. All lessons are blessings for those with eyes to see and ears to hear.

Lessons are priceless angels who come to teach people, so one should be grateful for the lessons, which is to be grateful for the mistakes. When one understands this concept, they become compassionate of the mistakes of others. Love is the behavior of compassion.

Compassion makes life easier, for love is the meaning of life and compassion is love's liberation.

Everything one did not do correctly yesterday they can correct today. One can take other's mistakes personally, but no one makes a mistake on purpose.

They did not know. People slip, a temporary moment of spiritual amnesia where they had forgotten what the upmost essence of love truly looks like.

To take something personal is to punish thyself for the sin of another.

Perhaps they never saw the upmost essence of love. One cannot expect another to behave in a way in which that person has never seen. If one wants the world to function a certain way, they must be that example for the world, and first show them.

A slip is an opportunity to learn, and only by picking one-self up will they learn. You may only show them what it looks like to stand.

Nobody can pick another up, only they can make the decision to get up and try another way. If thou were to open a caterpillar's cocoon to help it out, it would never become a butterfly.

Don't simply try again, try again in a different way. One can only learn by self-reflection, they cannot learn by projection. If anybody else picks them up, it does not make them stronger, so they will continue to slip for as long as they seek outside of them self for that which they already contain. Eventually one may learn to walk without slipping, but only if they love them self enough to forgive them self for their own faults, rather than blaming others.

Personal accountability is the key to strength. It hurts, but this is when pain is a friend. Life is not meant to be easy; if it were, it would become old and boring fast.

Nobody came here to be perfect, people come here to learn. The need for perfection is of the ego, as is the need for knowing. The desire to know should be replaced with the desire to learn.

Zen masters do not know everything; they learn everything. That is why they are Zen, because they are always open to receive, always open to learning.

Blocking the truth is a form of resistance that causes stress and anxiety. Blocking information can appear as a defense mechanism, it is the ego's way of saying, "I already know".

There is only one sin; to withhold love. All sin starts with the absence of discernment. To not discern is to not love the self. All other sin falls under the lack of love. As one exercises discernment they evolve in wisdom, and life improves in every way as a result.

Surrender into the unknown and open up to learning; thy Zen awaits thee in the frightening unknown. Fear is the light at the top of the lighthouse, follow it.

One will never find zen in a substance or a person, in money, nor in any other thing. They will only find zen inside of them self. Zen is what happens when ye stop resisting the learning. Learn from everything. No being is too young, weak, insignificant, or foolish to teach the wise. The wise teach them self all things through all things.

Life is practice, the practice for practice. Life is not the practice for perfect; life is the practice for more practice. Perfect already exists. Perfection exists in the heart, whenever one is there, all is seen as perfect. The practice of life never ends. The process is the practice and life is the process. The process is the mastery of allowing life to be practice rather than trying to make everything perfect, see that it is already perfect.

All of life is practice, so, one can remember to forgive them self and to forgive others, just as they would have others forgive them. Forgive others in life just as thou would forgive them in practice. When one takes life too seriously, they become rigid, and forgiveness becomes difficult. That which is rigid breaks under pressure. Life always brings pressure during the universe's contraction.

No one struggles with the same internal battles; therefore no one can fully understand the afflictions of another. Forgiveness is the key to freedom.

Oneness is forgiving all others for their sins. One couldn't possibly understand unless they could walk a mile in the shoes of another, and if they were to walk a mile in the shoes of another then they would understand. You might as well skip the mile and just go straight to understanding. The system is designed to keep one from knowing, so that one may surrender to the unknown and in doing so return home.

It is easy to declare that someone else is wrong. In fact, this is what the ego wants; by making someone else wrong, the ego has automatically made itself right in its mind.

Forgiveness is an ego death, which is why it is so difficult. Forgiveness does not require one to keep the person who wronged them in their life. Forgiveness does not require one to keep the person who hurt them in their life. Forgivingness requires only that one releases the person who hurt them from condemnation and takes responsibility for how they manifested the experience of them into their own reality.

The ego cannot handle forgiveness, which is why being hurt is actually a blessing, because being hurt gives people the opportunity to forgive, which as an ego death, is an ascension catalyst.

There is no need to thank people for hurting you. Simply forgive them, thank the universe for delivering a challenge, and thank thy self for passing the challenge by choosing love. Forgiveness does not require ye tell the other person thou forgive them either. Forgiveness is a personal task and is in no way deemed complete by any type of feedback from the outside world. Thou willst for sure experience positive feedback, but feedback is not required.

One can set an affirmation for a better life before falling asleep, in their sleep they may enter into a new portal and be reborn every day. Regardless of what happened yesterday, today it can be made right, by forgiveness. One only slips so that in pulling themselves up, they can pick others up with them. A person doesn't just slip for them self, we slip for one another. Life is like an ice-skating ring, and discernment are the blades on thy skates. Sharpen the blades of discernment with practice, and do not blame others when thou falleth. Hold one another's hand, and do not blame them if they fall and pull thee down. Simply get up together and learn from the experience. Others will learn by watching thy ways.

Nobody's opinions have any negative, or positive, impact on a wise person's reality. The wise do not concern with how other people speak of them or think about them. Only by attaching to the opinions of others are those opinions made real.

Those who try to curse thee are actually cursing themselves and blessing thy life. Only the opinions one has over himself can negatively or positively impact their reality. Others may shift their reality – shifts in life are inevitable – but the direction of that shift is determined by whether one views it in a positive light or casts it into the darkness.

Any time one condemns something to the darkness, they shackle them self. So, understand as much as possible. One can only love themself to the extent that they understand that which exists outside of their self. To understand is to stand under another, lifting them up in support of their awakening. When you say, "I understand", know that this is a declaration to forgive them. Even if you don't understand, say "I understand" as an affirmation, and let that I am statement blossom into reality. One does not need to understand in order to say they understand, they only need to make the decision to understand and let their own words be the affirmation to plant that seed of love into the ether fields of the universe.

Unconditional love is acceptance without the ability to understand. Unconditional love is the most powerful force in the universe. Uni meaning one, and verse meaning a rhythmic harmony. There is only one sound of the universe, and that sound is om. All things work together, harmoniously, through the sound of om. The om frequency is oneness consciousness, the understanding that all things work together to support the greater good, the greater God, the one true I Am, that is all things. Oh my God (om eye God). Visualize what thou willst attract into an om and it will come to thee.

Love is compassion in the midst of pain. Love is the willingness to die for what one believes in. Love is the willingness to live for what one believes in, and that's what makes love unstoppable. The dream is short and fast, but there is nothing worth dying for other than love, because love is the only thing worth living for. Death is a transformation. Death is the end of one dream and the beginning of another. What people call "death" is simply a portal into a new life. Death is not to be feared, death is the orgasmic dive into the unknown. Prepare for dying daily, with the sound of om.

9 RELATIONSHIPS

*To speak your truth is not enough, you
must live your truth.*

When ye start taking better care of thyself, ye
stop needing so much from others. There was a time
when slavery and murder was legal, then a time
when the suppression of women was common, and
now we must accept that we live in a time where
child abuse is normal. It is not natural to force a child
stand in line, raise their hand before speaking, sit in
doors all day, learn fleeting topics will fail them in
the real world, and respond to their questions with
"because I said so". It is written, "Lest ye behave as
children ye shall not enter the kingdom of heaven",
yet everyone is trying to make children act as adults.
That makes no sense.

We must trust that children are the closest to
God, and thus know what is right before adults
poison them with sugar, negative belief systems,
video games and media.

As adults the lack of self-love comes from one's
belief that they do not deserve happiness. As
children, some people were made to believe their
natural instincts were wrong. At some point it

became no longer acceptable to be happy for no reason, and children needed to earn their happiness by doing things like get good grades in classes they would never again remember and have no need for in the real world.

If those children did not do what adults ordered them to, they were punished, grounded, or in some other way not allowed to be happy. But grades mean nothing to a child, so from the child's perspective it seems as if they must earn their happiness by pleasing others. This is how people pleasers are made.

Children repeatedly hear the word "wrong", each time they make a mistake. They come to believe they are wrong, just as a pet comes to believe its name by saying it over and over again. As children, some people were taught that in order to be accepted, they need to earn acceptance by being better than the children around them. Those with the highest grades earn the most acceptance from the adults. All children are worthy of acceptance.

Children don't care who founded America because in their heart of hearts they know they are being lied to anyway. What happed 100 years ago doesn't matter to a child, what matters is what is happening today.

Now, as an adult, some people still believe they need to earn their happiness and acceptance, so they try to prove themselves to others. Such behavior would only achieve the opposite, coming across as insecure, or arrogant, and the rejection this behavior manifests only reinforces their belief that they are not worthy of acceptance and happiness. When someone acts arrogant, know it is only because they are trying to earn thy approval and tell them that they are worthy.

Some adults work so hard, even though it takes them further and further away from happiness, sometimes, they forget to love themselves.

Nobody needs to earn their happiness. All beings were born with happiness. Happiness belongs to each individual, and it resides inside of everyone at all times. Society has programmed some people to believe that if they are happy, but have nothing, then they are crazy. As if one should not be happy unless they have something to be happy about. They live as if one should need a job, house, car, family, and friends in order to deserve being happy, and if one is happy without those things, then they have lost their mind and should be treated as a sick person, or an outsider.

Actually, none of those things bring happiness, and can result in the opposite of happiness if those things were formed from the need to be happy rather than from service of one's spiritual gifts. When you have nothing, you feel like you have everything.

Standing between people and true happiness is self-doubt. Worries and limiting beliefs are the spawn of doubt. Fear and doubt are as real as love and faith. They are as real as one makes them. All these beliefs surrounding what one deserves stem from stories they have been sold since birth, that have been deeply programmed into their subconscious mind.

All that is real is energy, the moment, and one's spiritual gift. How one uses the moment, and their energy to serve God through their spiritual gifts is what fills them with happiness. Everything else is story and illusion. The stories one chooses to carry depend on how they feel about them self and how they view them self. The stories one chooses to believe paint their reality. Tell thyself positive stories about thyself and about others at all times.

Bless thy food to bless thyself because medicine is poison at the wrong dosage and poison is medicine with the right affirmation.

Prayer speaks to the power that flows through all things, giving everything life. Oneness is the container of that power. All beings are meant to be grateful at all times for the life force flowing through them, and to show gratitude by the worship of oneness. Not worshipping once a week at a designated location, but worshipping constantly, within every moment of every second.

One's body is the church, and their awareness is the worshipper. By worshiping all forms of life, and all forms of matter, one brings honor and health to their self. Worship is the key to life. Life will keep those who worship it youthful and will take care of them.

It is not enough to just speak thy truth, thou shalt live thy truth. There are many distractions in life, but fear is the root cause of all distractions.

It can sometimes be easy to become distracted by people, situations, disease, drama, jobs, relationships, the desire for relationships, and to believe that it is these things which hold ye back from success, but actually these things are only manifestations of you holding thyself back from achieving success. When ye switch the switch, thou seest these things are actually propelling thee forward. People carry the story that something is holding them back, in order to avoid change. It is the excuses that hold people back from achieving their greatest success in life, not the things people believe are holding them back, but the beliefs in and of themselves.

As a crutch, limiting beliefs function to keep people in a place of normality, where they are not presented with the opportunity to stand out, change, grow, be ridiculed, or dive into the unknown. Some people are afraid that if they are to change and grow beyond the norm, people might exile them from the tribe.

This tribe mentality roots back for thousands of years when standing outside of the small tribe's norm meant banishment from the tribe, and thus death. But now that is not the case, yet people still hold this fear of rejection within their DNA.

The world has changed in such a way that one no longer must change to meet the world's standards, and thou may allow the world to change to meet thy standards instead.

If a few people are not calling thee crazy, thou art selling thyself short. Only after transmuting one's fears and limiting beliefs into risks and inspirations, may they see that the very things they thought were holding them back were actually propelling them forward. Obstacles are opportunities.

The way eye see it, there are three types of relationships:

The first is the soul mate. One may be their own twin flame. Every soul mate prepares one for that divine, eternal, unconditionally loving relationship with them self. Every being in existence has soul, and all soul comes from the same source, thus all beings are soul mates. All beings are light beings, for all things come from the light. Even demons are light beings.

Demons are light beings that challenge ye to become thy greatest version of self by overcoming their tricks. The devil is the master of tricks. God first said let there be light, right, so all things in existence came from that light. Even the name Lucifer means Light Bearer because Luz in Spanish means light.

A twin flame is a soul mate that triggers you to grow by shining light on all of thy demons. A twin flame can be a lover, a family member, a friend, a co-worker, a pet that pisses you off sometimes, or anyone, but there is always a magnetism that causes you to stay even though it is uncomfortable. What the twin flame relationship teaches is patience, forgiveness, and understanding.

A soul flame is a passionate, fiery, romantic connection that is fast, easy, and will/should not last forever. Soul flames serve to muse spiritual gifts and get one across their comfort zone in a way that is inspiring. But the soul flame connection lacks the foundation required for a long lasting relationship, and if it was long lasting it would be too much of a distraction for you to serve God with the spiritual gifts the soul flame inspired to bring out of you, which would be self-destructive. Some co-dependent relationships are the result of soul flames not letting each other go when their time has expired. Like drinking rotten milk simply because it was so good when it was good, co-dependent relationships make people sick. The soul flame relationship allows us to manifest better music, work harder at our careers, create a new product, improve our bodies through fitness and eating healthier, or in some other way transmute that fire into creation.

After enough twin flame and soul flame connections, one may arrive at the place of divine unconditional love within them self, as their own twin flame and soul flame. This is when their reflection will manifest in form, mirroring that divine love they have actualized within them self. This reflection is the twin soul.

Once one meets their twin soul, they will discover that they are their best friend, and perfectly align with them in every chakra as well as in destiny. The twin soul relationship is harmony for one has found harmony within them self. Together, twin souls build the lives of their dreams. There is no "you complete me" for one is already complete. There is no 50-50, for they are already 100% in and of their selves. The twin soul relationship is 100-100. They both bring so much to the table that anything is possible.

One must not search for their twin soul, or it will keep them from having 100% of their focus invested in their own growth, which is required to become the version of self-necessary to attract their twin soul. Whether or not one attracts their twin soul is irrelevant because by the time they do they are so happy alone that they don't need anyone else. One cannot find a twin soul. If it is meant to be it is dependent upon one's destiny. Thus, the phrase, if it is meant to be it will be.

What you stop searching for outside of thyself, ye discover inside. Once ye have discovered that energy inside thyself, the universe presents it in a tangible form, outside, as a reflection of thee. Once thou hast become whole and complete, so will thy relationships become complete and whole. As above, so below.

Relationships are reflections, so one who wants better relationships can only achieve this by becoming a better person.

If one is lonely, by serving others they may

transcend loneliness. One who helps themselves to loving thoughts changes their vibration and sees love around them.

Hormonal shifts follow changes in thoughts, and one becomes more attractive to potential love interests, even on a chemical level. Pheromones are the body's ability to create chemicals that match the blueprint of thy thoughts to attract others who have the blueprints thou need for the sake of thy evolution. The body is a manifestation of the spirit, which is a manifestation of the soul. Everything is a cascade.

Loneliness may be frightening at first, because the human is not designed to be alone forever. But solitude is temporary, and loneliness is a state of mind. To accept the possibility of being whole alone, can make one feel like they will never have a partner. Yet, the opposite is true. Once you become whole alone, more people are attracted to you.

Attracting the right partner should not require any trying whatsoever. Attracting the right partner only requires one to be present enough to feel and sense their desires. Trying is not doing and doing is not being. What one wants to experience, they must first become. As one's vibration rises, people begin to feel so good around them that they become energetically attractive; true attraction is energetic affinity, not physical. Physical attraction is just a distraction.

Discernment must be mastered as one's vibration

increases, for all people want to be in high vibrational fields, but some only want to align with their field for long enough to feed on their energy source. If one does not practice discernment, lower vibration beings will syphon their energy, leaving them vibrationally lower again.

Exercise is critical for attracting the right partner, because exercise keeps vibrations high. Exercise is not about the way one looks; it is about the way they feel. Exercise every day, moderately and consistently. Exercise comes from to exit, or to out bad vibes. That's why it's called a workout. But it is said that all medicine is poison and all poison is medicine, the only difference is the dosage and the intention.

One who over exercises, finds their vibration even lower than before they started. Over exercising is due to the attachment to results, rather than for the sake of health. Attachment to any result is draining. Attachment to results is an entity in one's field convincing them that they are not enough as they are.

Holding too many expectations exhausts people. Those who release the attachments to results are then free to be present. Attachments to results can lead people to trying too hard, or even stop them from beginning in the first place. When one tries too hard at anything, spirit is blocked from flowing through them naturally. One who tries becomes stuck, and only by releasing expectations may they unstick themself. All forms of greatness come from the natural flow of spirit, which is made possible only by doing what one loves.

What you love is the thing you would do if money did not exist. To find thy calling, just follow thy heart as if money did not exist.

Spirit is only blocked by the mind, where all the goals live. Spirit is present in the now, but goals are of the future. The is no need to interrupt the perfect flow of the universe with plans.

Balance is being in the present while preparing for the future. Once people stop caring so much about finding a partner, and direct their attention inward, the universe delivers an abundance of people wanting to be their partner. And so, it is that in this way beggars can't be choosers.

Relationship is the greatest teacher. The most important relationship is the relationship with self. Learning happens on its own. When people do not enjoy the learning, they become tense, and the growth stops. Progression happens in the enjoyment of the process.

Learning can hurt, so be gentle with those who are in the process of learning. Forgive them, for they do not know. They are all learning, so forgive them all. In forgiving others, ye free thyself.

Consciousness is not generated in the brain. Consciousness is received by the brain, then perceived by itself. It doesn't begin in the brain; that is only where the perception of consciousness, in human form, begins. Consciousness will live on, even after the brain is gone. The brain is a device for receiving consciousness and projecting it into the realm, or matrix, that the human form is designed to experience.

Energy carries consciousness, and consciousness is the awareness of the frequency of that energy which resides somewhere along a spectrum ranging from infinitely high to nonexistent.

Nature built in a mechanism that causes people to feel like they need the opposite sex, for the sake of procreation. Consciousness overrides this mechanism. God Consciousness is not just being aware of God's voice, it is being aware of one's self, and true nature.

If a man withholds from ejaculation, he overrides nature. By storing his seed, he is made stronger and more youthful every day. The alkaline minerals, and prana of his seed will restore his glow, his energy, and make him more attractive, confident and powerful. If he should waste his seed then he is wasting his life.

A true king is still a king, even after man robs him of his crown, for a true king is not crowned by man, but by God. Nobody can remove a king's crown, except himself. A king is the greatest servant of all men. A king does not live for himself, but for others.

Royalty does not eat from silver spoons, while those around them starve. A true king eats with his fingers, teaches others how to eat with their fingers also, and lends the silver spoons to those unable to learn how to eat with their fingers. At the tip of the fingers are censers that trigger the release of specific enzymes needed to digest the exact foods handled. To eat from a silver spoon is detrimental to one's growth, not beneficial. Knowledge is at the fingertips of those who serve, ignorance is spoon fed to laziness.

Those who serve are crowned by God, those seeking to be served are crowned by man.

Service to the world is service to self, for all human beings were born to make the world a better place. Nobody owes their life to another. The only person one owes their life to is them self. Those who walk away from that which hold them back are loyal to the one thing they owe their life to, the self.

Bliss is the responsibility of each individual for themselves. One thing keeping people from experiencing bliss together is taking things personal. Another is people not allowing each other to be themselves. Blissness is never taking anything personal, like the saying, it's not personal, it's blissness.

Each person owes it to them self to follow their own heart straight to the heartbeat of the earth. The beat of thy drum is the beat of thy heart, walk to that. In the heart resides everything one could ever truly want or need. The real gold.

Thy heart holds the seed to thy destiny. The cure to misery is service to the world, its price is freedom. One cannot truly serve others if they do not have freedom within themselves. By freeing oneself, from their mind, they are made able to serve others. When one allows them self to truly see others, they become finally able to see them self.

If ye find thyself feeling lack, ask ye what have thou to give, and then start giving that. One may find that in return, the universe blesses them with even more to give. Service is how one can alchemize emptiness into wholeness.

Be the calm within the storm. Humans are the greatest capacity to feel emotion of all the beings in the Universe but feeling emotional does not mean one is emotional. One is not emotion but is at the center of the emotion. Emotion is just as much within you as it is around you, but emotion is not you. Thou art the awareness of emotion.

Rather than saying, "I am sad", one may say, "I am observing sadness within me." Thinking this way may allow one to communicate with emotion, find out why it has come, and how it is here to help.

The key to successful communication is non-reaction, the state of being attached to the moment while remaining detached from the outcome. Once one has mastered non-reaction, they may be their true self in all situations, not letting circumstances change them. But as circumstances change, so will the self. The true self is neither rigid nor flexible, but it just simply is the isness of all things.

People receive what they prepare for, because it is the preparation for that experience that manifests its formation into reality.

There is a fine line between complacency and optimism. Whatever can go right will go right, for those who believe.

Balance these truths; love without discernment is dangerous, prepare for the best and hope for the even better and awareness is the key to all things.

The only job light has is to shine in the darkness. In facing the darkness within oneself, one becomes a beacon of light and a conduit of that divine source known as God. Not until one illuminates within them self may they shine for others.

The purpose of the darkness is to hold space for the expansion of light. So do not fear the darkness, allow it to inspire thy light. If ye fear the darkness thou becometh the darkness, for the essence of darkness is fear.

We are called Hue-mans because our purpose is to spread light. Whatever thy spiritual gift is, is thine you-nique way of spreading light. If ye follow thy spiritual gifts thou art destined to become madly successful, or happily successful, rather. Humans are meant to collaborate, not to be at war with one another.

To make peace with the world, one must start with themselves, then share that peace with others. One cannot share what they do not have. One cannot share love, if they do not possess it within them self. Ye cannot bring peace to the world, until thou hast made peace with the world.

Life is the dream of a journey. The beginning of the journey is the most exciting time. The middle is challenging, and the end is enlightening.

Micro-dose on nothingness, for nothing can ever fill one's cup as much as space can. Learn from space, for only silence has more to teach than space. Fasting is essential to spiritual growth; it is only in the space that one can expand. Ascension is expansion. The more space you give thyself, the more thou groweth.

All spirits, all experience, is here to serve the greater good of all. The struggle is only real for those who choose to believe in struggle. The moment one realizes it is their mind that creates the stories they call struggle, they begin to consciously manufacture new stories, that are beautiful. Even the struggle becomes beautiful.

Nothing can always go thy way, but only when thou hast no way, can nothing always go thy way.

Depression is the state of going from asleep to lucid. The moment one realizes they are dreaming, the show ends, along with the pain. One becomes lucid, and able to shape their own reality. Rather than being the actor, they become the observer and the creator. The actor is great but comes with the price of pain.

The awakening period feels like a depression. To realize that the matrix we live in was created by God, for God's experience. We are all fragments of that one. To navigate the matrix doors and keys are necessary, but those tools were not handed over so we must create them. Doors and keys are necessary for shaping realities. Doors are beliefs and truths are the keys. But truth and reality is different for truth is of the spirit realm and reality is of the physical. All that is real may not be truth.

Everything one experiences is here to serve them as a catalyst to their awakening. Pain teaches people to surrender their need for control.

Each moment of frustration teaches patience. Patience is the ability to accept what one may not understand.

Each moment of fear teaches courage. Courage is to remain constantly leaning into fear, rather than fighting or running. Courage is doing what frightens you most, so fear is good.

Each moment of insecurity teaches confidence. Confidence is to embrace that which is seemingly less than.

Pain arrives as a guide into greater states of happiness and freedom. With these truths, barriers become blessings. It is never easy to see in a storm, unless thou art the eye of the storm. When it rains, clouds block the light; anger or sadness can so easily ensue. When the clouds clear the rainbow becomes visible; but the rainbow was always there, you just couldn't see it without the rain. So be grateful for the rain, plus it shows up to wash away the pain.

10 MANIFESTING

Reverence is seeing the sacred in all things.

When it seems as though things are falling apart, they are actually coming together, like a puzzle. It's all divine, all the time. Those seemingly chaotic moments are the moments of clearing. The old must be cleared away, for the new to come through. If one is upset about circumstances, the truth is that a better situation is on its way.

Be as a lotus. The lotus was born in the depths of the dark mud. As a sprout it moved through the darkness towards the surface, not knowing which way was up and which way was down but seeking only the light.

Never becoming distracted by the darkness, it remained loyal to its calling, so it reached the surface, awakened, and blossomed as the highest vibration plant on the planet. Even higher than a rose, for a lotus is a water rose.

Not all plants grow in the mud, many other plants would be consumed by the mud's darkness. The lotus is to plant realm what the diamond is to mineral realm. The lotus is as strong as it is beautiful, as dense as it is expansive.

In Buddhism the golden lotus represents enlightenment. In-light-in-meant. It was meant for the light all along, not because its path was easy, but because its path was difficult. The lotus was not born in the palace. It was born in the mud, its path was lonely and dark, and it found its way to the palace by pursuing only the light. In rising for the darkness into the light it became so inspiring that it was chosen by royalty.

The darkness tries to convince people that they don't deserve the light. If the darkness succeeds in that, self-destructive behaviors ensue. That is how people get lost in the mud. Reverence, forgiveness, gratitude, and love make up the path towards the light.

Reverence is seeing the sacred in all things. Forgiveness is releasing others and accepting responsibility for thyself. Just as with great power comes great responsibility, so with great responsibility comes great power.

Forgiveness is the gateway to empowerment. One may only step into their power, through forgiving others. Gratitude is being fully present in the moment, with honor for whatever comes up. Love is having so much loyalty to the light that one does not even engage with the darkness, even when darkness surrounds them. Love is light.

Forgiveness is the thing you do before you give. Mastering being human is about forgiveness, not about perfection. Truth is a release. As long as one condemns anybody, they hold themselves hostage to their own demons. Forgiveness will set them free, for forgiveness is the truth, and the truth will always set you free.

Light is a friend of the darkness. One gives light to all of the spirits that greet them, even though some seem frightening, and that is how they recruit friends, by transmuting enemies. They know that all spirits are here to lead them toward their greatest version of self, for their affirmation is to be the light. In being the light, they only attract positive things. One can attract whatever they think about, but typically people are not aware of their thoughts, the Iceberg Principle.

By following one's heart, they find their passion. By remaining loyal to their passion, regardless of what others say, one finds their destiny. Only an individual can know what's right for them self.

If someone calls someone crazy, and they believe them, they may be listening to a crazy person. Crazy people drive people crazy. Place just one bad apple in a bucket of good apples, they will all spoil. Similarly, place one crazy person in a room with sane people, they will all go crazy; eye call this the Apple Effect, and it's how conspiracy theories, lies, and toxic rumors so easily spread. The apple effect is the cause of hysteria.

In being oneself, as odd as it may seem, one permits others to be themselves too. That is a beautiful thing.

The physical realm is a metaphor for what lies beneath the surface. What lies beneath the surface is 99.9% of reality, iceberg, one must see it to change it. One may not manifest what they want until they allow themselves to dive deep enough into the darkness to discover what is keeping them from already having it.

One who gives implicitly never worries about them self; as long as they keep taking care of the world, the world takes care of them. When people stop giving, they start worrying, for life is just like everything else... one may only get out of it what they put into it.

The amount of success one will experience in any field is directly proportional to their willingness to learn. By remaining coachable through taking nothing personal, one is destined to go farther than those who become defensive. Those who want to grow must not be defensive or think they already know.

There is no voice that one cannot learn from. There is no person who is not a teacher. Everything is showing everyone something about them self that they need to see in order to move to their next stage of spiritual evolution. One who heals them self becomes a healer. One does not become a healer by trying to become a healer, one becomes a healer by healing them self. So only wounded people can become healer, therefore, never judge a person who has harmed another, for a wounded person can't not wound other people, the Apple Conspiracy. A leader is someone who inspires by example. A healer is one who steps out of the way and allows others to heal themselves.

Fear is the shadow of love. People love what they think they understand and fear what they think they do not understand. People love what they are familiar with and fear what is unfamiliar.

It is not the substance that determines whether or not it's a drug, but how the substance is yoused. You are the substance you think you are taking.

One can be in love with toxicity, only because they are familiar with it. A person who is familiar with abuse, will fear a healthy relationship, because they are unfamiliar with healthy relationships, thus do not understand its nature. One familiar with abuse, is likely to turn a healthy relationship, into a toxic relationship, simply because toxicity is what they are used to. Abuse, is to use, therefore any form of taking advantage of someone is abuse. One should not use any substance but should have a healthy symbiotic relationship with it.

The Ego tries to make people fight against or run from what they fear. A person who is unfamiliar with healthy relationships, and follows his or her Ego, will run from a healthy relationship, or fight the person who is healthy in that relationship. Fighting in and of itself is not abuse, the nature of abuse is to use someone. Those who have been abused, and have not yet healed, are likely to imagine they are being abused even if they are not.

One who has been abused will project abuse onto someone who may be very good to them, and may accuse that person of abusing them, simply because they are used to it.

One manifests by seeing, believing, and feeling. Two people may walk into the same circumstances and walk out with completely different stories. They will both recreate the stories they came up with, whether positive or negative.

Acceptance is the key to joy. One may not love their circumstances right now, but the amount of joy they can create, is directly proportional to the amount of acceptance they can summon.

One may not have chosen their circumstances, and those circumstances may not be their preference, but that doesn't mean they can't accept them. If one accepts their circumstances, joy will be the immediate result.

To society, joyful people in unfavorable circumstances appear crazy, but that is only because society does not understand joy. Society only understands goals, but the goal-oriented mind is not a joyful mind. A joyful mind is childlike. One can manifest everything they want but having all those things may only give them more to worry about.

When one accepts their circumstances, they feel a release from lack. Happiness is carried by abundance. If one is happy, it makes no difference whether they chose their circumstances or those circumstances chose them. Happiness is the point.

You are not what anyone else thinks you are, they are what they think you are. Thus, judge not, that ye not be judged. Judgment is the evidence that one does not understand. The judgment of anything opens the portal to the experience of that thing, for the sake of understanding.

Nobody is better or worse than anybody. To praise anyone as better than another, or to belittle anyone as worse than another, is ignorance. To worship anyone as better than the self is a delusional, for what one sees in another is alive within him.

The human race is one being; the human being is one body. It is not a human race, it is a human journey, and instead of competing we are collaborating.

All human beings are varying reflections of the same being. The human spirit is one spirit, just as the animal spirit is the spirit to that animal.

Honesty is the key to discernment. One must be honest with them self. Many project the qualities they are seeking to find, into the people they meet. If one desires to find a reflection with certain qualities, the only way to manifest that is to first develop those qualities within them self.

Those who love themselves are very slow, patient, and careful with who they share their life with. It is okay to withdraw with love. If one has self-love, to pull back may come naturally. Stepping back can actually be stepping forward.

Hear people's words and listen to their actions.

Wait to see that a person's words align with their actions, before trusting them.

Nothing can ever hurt you as much as the fear of being hurt can. The fear of being hurt can rob ye of thy entire life. In order to manifest one must take risk. Leap and the net will appear.

Meditation is a mind-body vacation. The answers to all questions reside in silence. One may find that silence when they enter into the theta state. The silence tells people everything they need to know. That is why people fear the silence, it changes them. One can either know, or they can let go, and grow.

Life is a journey of the unknown. Life is a journey of the un-own. Let it go. The things they own end up owning them. First one accepts what is not meant for them, then they receive what is meant for them, not the other way around. The blessings of the universe are earned by the acceptance of what is and what is not.

There is no benefit in the avoidance of depth. There is no need to hide truth from people to avoid hurting their feelings. Truth will only trigger growth, in that way, pain can be a friend.

Loving is not going to harm anyone; if it hurts, it's only making them stronger. But fear of pain can keep people from loving.

There is no such thing as bad. There is only good and not so good. That which is perceived as bad, is simply the absence of good. There is only God and the absence of God, light and the absence of light.

Darkness does not exist, only light exists. Darkness is simply the void.

The absence of God is the void. The void is nothing; that is, darkness. One can put anything into the darkness. One can even put more darkness into the darkness, which is to expand the void, creating only more pain and misery through the perpetuation of negativity.

People put more darkness into the darkness by creating victim stories and dramatic endings instead of positive conclusions. They add more distortion, which is suffering, to the distortion and suffering. One could just as easily add truth, which is positivity. When one puts light into the darkness, something real comes of that. Reality is healing, distortion is disease. Everything worth doing, is hard before it becomes easy. Anger is punishing thyself for the mistakes of others. A pun is a trick, and the desire to punish anything stems from delusion. If one puts more nothing into the nothing, their life force will be drained, and they will drain those around them, like a black hole. But if they put something, light, into the nothing, they will be charged, and they will charge those around them, like the sun. The sun brings life, and so does light. Thus, why negative people drain you and positive people give you energy.

Faith is the seed of manifestation. If it is not fun anymore, it is not worth doing. One cannot do their best if they do not enjoy the activity. There is something out there that is fun, which one will be more successful at than whatever they think they need to do for money. The word fundamental carries with it two parts, fun and mental, because the foremost important aspect of any activity is that it is fun for the mind. People are successful at what they enjoy most, because it is those activities, they can really set their mind to, and the mind is a powerful machine.

Everything in the world is a distraction. Heaven is within each being. One will not find heaven in anything outside of them self. Go inward, by releasing all distractions. Let all things be, as they are, without attaching to them and without judging them.

All things come to go. A wise person loves people while they are present and does not let fear stop them from letting them go. Meditate on being everything and nothing at the same time. Everything one could ever possibly want, and dream for, already lives within them.

As one heals others, so they are healed. One cannot always change their circumstances, but one can always allow their circumstances to improve their character. By focusing on how ye respond to thy circumstances, and by intending to handle them in a virtuous manner, ye may allow even the unfavorable circumstances, to make thee a better person.

11 POWER

Those who desire to be great are met with collapse, and those who desire to serve are met with greatness.

If it's not meant to be it cannot be, if it is meant to be it can't not be. So, rest easy. Good people lead good lives.

Surrender is not accepting defeat. Surrender is choosing faith over hope. Surrender all worries to the divine. One surrenders when they are ready to receive. The key to surrender is faith.

The key to joy is surrender. One taps into the flow state, by mastering what was once a challenge, that they always loved.

There is a proverb that says a man sat by a tree meditating for months. One day Buddha came passing by; when the man saw Buddha, he became very excited.

"Buddha!" the man shouted. "If I keep meditating like this, how long will it take for me to reach illumination?!"

Buddha responded, "If you keep meditating by that tree, like that? Ten lifetimes."

The man groaned with disappointment and went back to meditation. Buddha continued to walk through the forest. He crossed paths with a man who had been dancing by a tree for months, "Buddha!" The man shouted, "If I keep dancing by this tree like this, how long will it take for me to reach illumination?!"

Buddha responded, "If you keep dancing by that tree, like that...? 100 lifetimes". The man immediately shouted back at the Buddha, "AWESOME!!!", and at that exact instant, the man reached illumination.

It is not what one does, but how they do it that determines the success of their endeavors. Because finding joy is the greatest success there is. Joy is an even higher vibration than love, some say.

Bring a joyful nature to all endeavors. Do what you love, and thou shalt be destined for success. Fun is the fundamental objective of life. If one can't enjoy their work, it will be impossible for them to do their best.

The will of the heart space is the true source of power. The mind is fate to the blind. Love is the only true destiny, how one expresses love in their language is their signature, the will of their heart space. The only thing standing in the way of anyone and their greatest power is surrender. It seems ironic, that those who desire to be great, are met with collapse, yet those who desire to serve are met with greatness. But it is not ironic at all, it makes perfect sense. The only thing between one and their destiny is the goal-oriented mind.

A child does not say "When I grow up, I want to be a cowboy, fireman, ballerina, actor, doctor, singer" etc. because that is their destiny. Children say that stuff because they see it everywhere. People are born to love, create and play. It is the world that derails them. Children never say, "When I grow up, I want to be me." Or "What is growing up, and why would I ever do it?" Children say what they see.

The mind is a computer, it does not create energy; it is guided by awareness to direct energy. The mind exists for the purpose of calculation and projection. There must first be a projection, before there can be a reflection.

What thou seeth is a projection of what lives within thee, reflected back on a screen made of primordial ether.

The mind is like a horse, one must contain and train it if they desire to have direction. Until tamed, it runs wild causing destruction.

Mental discipline is the ability to control the mind. Train thy mind to surrender to what is. To find joy learn the difference between what you can control, and what you cannot; what you should control and what you should not.

Discipline is the key to achievement. The amount of achievement thou wilt experience in life is directly proportional to the amount of discipline thou canst embody. Even the sustainable embodiment of joy requires discipline.

Discipline is the ability to control thy mind. Practice self-mind control daily by creating imaginative objects, moving them, and alchemizing them into new objects and colors with thy imagination. Thy "image-eye-in-at-ion". Imagining a world where there is total peace and harmony will bring peace and harmony to thy cells.

There are miracles, mirror-calls, happening everywhere, but one can only see them by tapping into a frequency of gratitude. Listening to 444Hz will harmonize a person to feel gratitude from every cell of their being and draw towards them miracles from every direction of the universe, north, south, east, west, in, out below and above.

Sustaining balance between the mind and the heart space is essential for making healthy decision. One must not get so caught up in the desire for success, that they forget to love them self, and love all of life around them. For there can be no success without love.

If ye want to be successful, just do thy will, because nobody can do you better than you, and it's the path of least resistance. The will of thine own heart is the path that God created for thee.

Nobody has been bestowed with the blueprint of thy destiny other than thyself. It is common to look around and desire to emanate what works for others. But if a bird tried to become a fish it would drown.

We must learn to love failure if we are to

embrace the experience of life. Failure, as a concept, has been cast into the darkness, but failure is not bad; it is relative. One may fail at level ten, but only because they have failed at level ten do they succeed at level nine. Each new level requires a certain amount of failure to master, until thou may rise into the next level. If one should fear, resist, or resent failure, they would remain stuck where they are. As they say, still waters run dry.

The solution to dryness is learning to love, and even desire the experience of failure. Life is but a game. One who loves to fail as much as they love to win, has nothing to do in life other than to love. This is the way of children. The game is not played for the sake of winning, but for the sake of playing. Because children are so present with their play, the learning, new connections, and ultimately the mastery takes place naturally. Children do not try to learn, children learn simply because they do what organically interests them. It is written that unless we return to be like children we shall not enter the kingdom of heaven. To be childlike is simply to do what it is that you enjoy.

12 BLESSINGS

Nothing can be bad, if you allow it to
make you better.

The greatest of blessings are bestowed upon
those who take responsibility, response-ability,
for all things that happen in their life.

There is a story of a king who became vexed
because all the people in his kingdom blamed
him for every mishap in the land. One day, the
king decided to place a boulder in the middle of
the road.

The next day a line of angry people, a mile
long, came to complain about the boulder
blocking the road. This continued, day after day,
for weeks.

Eventually, a common peasant had finally
had enough of all the complaining and took it
upon himself to move the boulder.

To his surprise, as he shifted the stone, he
found a miracle under it. The king had placed a
giant bag of gold coins beneath the boulder.

There are blessings bestowed upon those
who take responsibility, for all things that

happen in their life. One can either complain, or they can make change. Make change, always, and it always starts within.

The mind is always at work; to turn it off will give it necessary rest, that is meditation. The mind is even at work while one sleeps. Just like turning off a computer, one must daily turn off the mind. If it becomes overworked, the mind will begin to make systematic errors. Only by adding meditation to one's life are they able to work smarter instead of harder.

When one maintains equilibrium between the heart space and the mind, all problems dissolve by themselves. The heart space does not refer to the physical heart organ; it refers to the chakra that manifested the heart organ. The heart space is intuitive. The heart space is connected to the same heart space of all nature.

Knowingness is not of the mind; knowingness is of the heart. Tap into the heart space by all things green to discover thy will. Harness the crown by all things violet to achieve thy destiny. Charoite is a destiny stone. The mind is a computer, control it, don't let it control thee.

All people are absolutely perfect. All people are also flawed, and it is their flaws that reflect their perfections. In loving that which is seemingly imperfect, one is proven perfect. One cannot be proven perfect, without loving that which the world deems imperfect. Flaws exist, to give reason for love. Flaws exist to allow people into the heart space.

In meditation, one finds eternal bliss, a light, that stays with them. Large amounts of turmeric and black pepper, gold, sun gazing, and fasting are tools that can be paired with meditation to open higher dimensional gateways within one's being, to give a sense of enlightenment.

Once a person has seen their light, they may carry it everywhere, or place it down. Your light is as loyal to thee as thou art to it. Discipline.

Time is the healer of all wounds, but it is also the source of forgetting. One must stay on their daily practice. Prior to enlightenment one chops wood and does chores, post enlightenment one still chops wood and does chores.

All experience leads to the knowledge of self, so there is no bad experience, for all experience makes one better if they choose to learn from it. Nothing can be bad that makes you better.

Few will want thy company, when thou need to be in company, and when thee finally become happy alone, everyone starts wanting thine company. A king is a man who has found his eternal fulfillment. A king sees a king from afar. A king sees not from his mind, but from his heart.

Kings congregate without proving themselves to one another, give, without asking for recognition, titles, or acknowledgement. Together, kings do great things for the world, in service to as many beings as possible.

One who bows down with an agenda to be praised, will be diminished further. When ye no longer desireth praise, that's when thou art praised.

Do not be fooled by the matrix, the may-trix, for it is built on backwards belief systems.

A queen does not need to prove herself worthy, neither to herself nor to anyone else, for a queen is already worthy to herself. If ye struggle with feelings of low self-worth, look to thy integrity.

Competition is a fallacy, there is no winner in a competition, only losers. Winners don't compete; winners collaborate. All humans on earth could very well collaborate; the only thing stopping humans around the globe from harmoniously collaborating is fear of loss. The unfortunate aspect of this is that people manifest what they fear just as they manifest what they love. The competition between nations, classes, religions, races, sexes and so on puts the world at a state of loss. Only by coming together may we all rise; only be rising together may we heal the Earth. Planet Earth has taken the toll for mankind's competitive design. The desire for more may put people in a state of willful destruction to achieve their goals by any means necessary, even if it means destroying the Earth in the process.

Goals can be okay, because life is an experience. Experience is only made possible by desire. One who births a new desire, or goal, is suddenly taken on a journey; that journey is the experience. This is why we are here; for experience. To remain detached, yet in a state of wonder is the primary objective; to be moved, rather than to move. We come from the spiritual into the physical to not forget our spiritual essence.

13 ALCHEMY

Life is a rebound, everything you put
out is bound to come back.

The human body takes in on average of 7% of its
mass per day. That means that 7% of the body's
mass is shedding per day. In a year one would have
an entirely new body. One may use this information
to change their body chemistry on a cellular level
within a short amount of time. Daily detoxing
consistency is key to fully optimizing cellular
turnover.

A famous study was done on water proving that
water reshapes itself according to the words you put
into it. Dr. Emoto wrote words in front of water and
took pictures of the molecules structure as they
changed over time. The water he put negative words
in front of became jagged and asymmetrical. The
water he put healing words in front of, such as "I
love you", became harmoniously symmetrical
embodiments of sacred geometry.

Our bodies are mostly water, so words have the
same effect on our cells. To say I love you to another
person is not a declaration of ownership or
attachments to expectation. To say I love you to

someone is simply to bless them.

There are only two types of sex. Sex is either tantric or it's toxic. Tantra is bringing presence to the present moment. Many people tap out during sex, rather than tapping in. Sex is the creative life force energy. Sex magic is a way of harnessing this energy for the cause of manifestation.

Emotion is energy in motion. Emotion, visualization and faith are the three keys to manifestation. Any emotionally charged activity can be used to manifest with visualization, purpose, and faith. Especially if the emotion of that activity is positive, blissful and (aura) gasmic.

One should abstain from ejaculation while practicing tantra, for injaculation is an expansion of the aura and awakening of the kundalini. Injaculation causes the kundalini to rush up the spine and explode through the crown. This sensation is similar to the kundalini awakening yet is specific to the crown.

Ejaculation causes an immediate expansion of the aura, followed by an implosion of energy. This implosion is due to the fact that physical energy is extinguished through the root chakra, leaving nothing to stabilizing the expansive explosion. Injaculation allows the body to save this physical energy, thereby amplifying and redistributing it.

There are several tools one may use to tap into tantra. Eye gazing, breath, stillness, the million-dollar point, and so on. How we do one thing is how we do everything, so tapping into tantric sex is the strongest way to harness a tantric life.

The ideal state of being is not one extreme nor the other, but the perfect harmony between both polarities. No form can be without thought and no thought can be without form. A being is a thought form. Even just a blade of grass is a thought form, both masculine and feminine.

Alchemy is the relationship between consciousness and matter. Alchemy is the understanding of how thoughts shift matter. The awakened mind has harmonized the balance of masculine and feminine energies within and without. They no longer see masculine nor feminine, but simply life.

To say feminine is not to say woman, and to say masculine is not to say man. Feminine and masculine are not genders, man and woman are genders. Feminine and masculine are energies. Men and women should not be attached to the ideas of what feminine and masculine is supposed to look like, for if they attach to man-made concepts, they will miss the natural flow of prana moving through them.

Notice the way a mother loves her baby. It is the greatest example of worship. She gives it life, and then she praises it, rather than expecting it to praise her for giving it life. That is humble.

When the masculine and feminine unite within one being there is eternal harmony, support, and power within the self...this is the awakening. The Awakening is achieved through Yoga, Alchemy, and awareness of the present moment.

An alchemist transmutes meaning from that which is ordinarily meaningless, transforms that which has no ordinary value into that which is extremely valuable. An alchemist finds the gold in the salt, turns the mercury into gold. Alchemy is transformation and transmutation. Transformation is harnessing energy to change form. Transmutation is harnessing awareness to change energy. Thus, transmutation is the beginning of transformation.

One must transmute, before they can transform. An alchemist is one who practices the state of transmute and transformation. It all starts the ion, transformation. The Egyptians turned mercury into gold using a mystery material, which was electricity. King Solomon made solid gold from ocean water by materializing the ormus. Jesus used yoga. An alchemist can take the trinity apart or put the trinity together.

Yoga is the fusion of soul, body and spirit. Living by the trinity is a sacred path. Sacred means to be aware of the oneness within all things. The trinity is the soul, body and spirit.

By letting go of the desire to reach a destination one is enabled to focus on the path. One who focuses on the path opens gateways for infinite energy to flow through him. This chi allows people to accomplish otherwise impossible tasks. With presence what was impossible becomes I'm possible. Attaching to any goal will block the flow of prana, for all goals are future based, detached from the present, and magic happens only in the present. Nature is magic. Nature is present, no goals, simply intuitive being. All goals are futile. One who gives up all goals becomes lighter and creates faster.

There is a story of a farmer who plowed the same fields his entire life. It was just him, his son and their horse on this farm, and they were dependent on that horse for their survival.

One day the son left the gate open and the horse ran away. The neighbors saw this happen and shouted to the farmer, "What terrible luck!" The farmer replied, "Maybe so, maybe not... we'll see."

A couple days later their horse returned home bringing wild horses with her. The neighbors saw this happening and shouted, "What great luck!" The farmer replied, "Maybe so, maybe not... we'll see."

Later that week the son was riding one of the horses, breaking her in, and she threw him to the ground, breaking his hip. The neighbors shouted to the farmer, "What terrible luck!" The farmer replied, "Maybe so, maybe not... we'll see."

A couple weeks later the national army came marching through the town and recruited every boy to fight in their war. They spared the farmer's son because he had a broken hip. The neighbors saw this and shouted at the farmer, "What great luck!" The farmer replied "Maybe, maybe not... who knows."

And so, it is that when ye change the way thou looketh upon things, the things thee looketh upon change. It might seem strange but use loving words and watch the atoms rearrange.

Holy is dedicating a purpose to that which is sacred. Holy is the process of showing up to the present moment in a humble manner. Humble is placing the self aside for the greater good of all.

Gratitude is the result of focusing on the path, releasing the desire to get somewhere or something out of the present moment. Presence is potential. By tapping into the present moment, one experiences an increase in awareness. Awareness is the key to all things. The more present one is, the more power they have over themself, thus the more power they have over their environment. As within so without.

Presence naturally harmonizes everything. By harmonizing both masculine and feminine energies one becomes whole with the self, which is to become one with their environment. The pendulum no longer swings. One is no longer in their environment and has become the environment.

That is the opposite of, "in the world but not of the world." Yet, both can be true. One can not only be in the world, but can also be one with the world, allowing all things to flow through them without attaching to any of it.

Unity consciousness is the understanding that to be the world is to be love. Influence is to no longer be only in the container, but to become the container. The holy trinity is bringing a sacred aspect to the mind, body and soul. Alchemy contains three components: Consciousness (soul-energy), Spirit (Ego-mind), and Body (vessel-matter).

An alchemist sees everything as soul, spirit, and body. The Spirit is the interpretation of the soul's experience of the body. So, as one changes the body, so changes they the Spirit. This is why natural remedies are made to change the vibration of one's body. By transmuting consciousness's experience of the body, the spirit is transformed. Some plants, and other gifts from the earth are spirit allies, like gold, frankincense, Egyptian blue lotus, rose and myrrh.

As this shift in interpretation forms new patterns in the body (brain[neuro-chemistry]), new and healthier patterns of thinking and behaving are habituated and permanently actualized within the body.

One could also change their mind to change their body. This is more challenging alchemy and requires mastery of illusion, it is to be a magician. Magic is the most advanced form of alchemy, but is always being done to some extent, implicitly. Mantras support one in changing the mind.

To change thy life, change thy mind and to change thy mind, change thy mantra. One can repeat a mantra such as, "I am happy.", until they start smiling. If ye repeat anything for long enough, thy mind begins to believe it. One can make a mantra whatever they want.

A positive mantra will have a permanent imprint on the body, just as smiling will make a permanent imprint on the mind's circuitry. The practice of smiling and neuro-linguistic programing can be utilized to reroute the brain's grooves.

The body is a tuning fork. One's posture sends signals into the universe which come back in the form of an external experience. This is why yoga involves posture. Facial expression is a form of posture too.

The posture first sends a signal to the brain, then the brain sends thoughts in the form of signals into the ether field. The universe responds by sending back evidence of what thou art thinking.

Everything one sees, hears, and believes is a reflection of their own thoughts, which are in turn reflections of their postures. Life is a rebound, everything you put out is bound to come back; eye call this the Rebound Effect. One who puts out hate is going to get hate. One who puts out love is going to get love.

The essence of neuro-linguistic programming, which is alchemy of the mind, is using language to change the brain pathways, which in turn changes one's life. One can start changing their life with neurolinguistics programming, or one can start with vibrational medicines, but it's best to start with both.

Ormus carries with it high vibrations that raise the frequency of one's vessel, allowing the being to experience more positive thoughts, thus attracting more positive things, circumstances, and situations into his reality. It also catalyzes the rate of karma (learning) and synchronistic phenomena (manifesting).

Ormus also synchronizes the masculine and feminine, the artistic and the scientific, the left and the right brain. This balance results in eternal union and harmony. It also awakens the theta state, which is the healing state of being where one becomes their own healer. Eternal union is unity consciousness, ormus consciousness is unity consciousness; oneness. That is why everyone is drawn to it. Having ormus in one's system will also make them more attractive, energetically.

The experience of increasing synchronistic phenomena is evidence of an increasing awareness.

Truly, all is one. Alone (all one). L(one)li(ness) is God consciousness. "Loneliness" is an illusive nightmare that stems from judgment, not letting others fully be themselves.

Alone, as a conceptual fallacy. There is nothing that stands alone, but things only appear to stand alone. Nothing is not connected to everything. Everything is everything. Therefore, everything is connected. One can feel emotions and think they are their own, but those emotions belong to everything. One just happens to be feeling them.

The substance of alchemy is change, the only constant in life is change. Thus, alchemy is life. Until the 1600s alchemy was used in the way that we now use the word chemistry. In Egypt Alchemy was the black arts, black meaning mystical or unknown.

Black is the color of neutrality, the womb, the zero point of creation. Alchemists wear black for out of the black can come anything.

Alchemy is a philosophy, older than religion, the one and final truth. Everything one sees is the result of alchemy unfolding.

Water is a liquid crystal. As a crystal water holds and catalyzes information. As a liquid water shapes itself according to the codes that have been placed into it by its observers and surroundings. Before drinking water, always tell it that "I love you". Always thank thy water, for bringing thee life.

Put gratitude into thy water, and thine water will put gratitude into thee. Put nothing into the water, and thy water remains blueprinted with the signatures of the chaos it journeyed through before reaching thee. Drinking the right water is the key to youthful aging.

Treat humans in the same way. The eyes cast codes upon everything they see. The human is over 60% water, and humans absorb these codes. Water does not discern; it simply changes form to align with whatever vibration it makes contact with.

Thy mitochondria do not trigger hunger. Parasites trigger hunger. If thou feel hunger, ignore it. Intuitive eating is not eating whatever thy body wants. Intuitive eating is eating according to the wants of thine cells. About 90% of the cells of thy body are foreign bacteria. It is your cells you want to feed, not theirs. In order to tap into the voice of one's own cells they must fast, cleanse and detox regularly.

Every cell of a person's body hears the thoughts of that person and shapes itself according to those thoughts. One may think negatively towards another person and think it's okay, but it is their own body who hears those thoughts, and becomes those thoughts, taking the toll for that person's negativity. To send a curse towards another, is to curse thyself first even greater. To send a blessing towards another, is to bless thyself even greater.

Change is inevitable. Things may seem good for now, but if one does not constantly work to make things better, life will corrode around them. Entropy is the natural result of complacency.

The mind is like a wild horse; control thy mind and it may take thee where thou art trying to go... love thy mind that it may take thee far beyond thy wildest dreams. To love the mind is singing to all of its fear. Reminding the mind that it's okay to be afraid, and it's okay to move through fear. Not feeling fear doesn't make a person courageous, it makes them unaware. Feeling fear then moving through it is what makes a person courageous.

In this physical realm one has an energetic imprint upon everything they see, touch and think about. Karma is the cause and effect of our action. Thought is action first and foremost. The future one experiences will be either as good, or as not so good as their karma. To remain in a state of reverence for all things ensures good karma. To think with love even upon those things which have caused you pain is your free will, and results in your ascension. The virtues are here to guide each individual towards ascension and it is when they look away from those virtues and fall into anger, jealousy, vengeance, greed, hate, or judgment that they experience descension only of themselves.

Seek only thoughts of love, acceptance, generosity, gratitude, compassion, and forgiveness and your happiness will be unstoppable. Success follows happiness. Generosity is letting things go. To truly let something go, without clinging, is to give. It is to give space, time and freedom. Humility allows for generosity. The humble are able to give because they are not crippled with a sense of entitlement. Gratitude is the result of generosity. As one gives, space opens up within themselves to receive, and the opening of that space feels like freedom to the self. People free themselves by freeing others, and gratitude is the feeling that results.

Wisdom is presenting one's self to inspire positivity out of others, for there is no other. The meaning of life is whatever you decide it is. Your life, your meaning. Life is your dream.

CLOSING

It is with reverent pleasure that I present you with this offering. You are as unique, magical and magnificent as all of the universe itself.

If you enjoyed Lucid Living, share it with others. We are here to inspire, so if this conversation has awakened a positive spirit within you, I welcome you to leave a review and to follow my journey on social media, @archerlove. Direct message me for collaborations, or to share your thoughts on this book. I do my best to respond to all of my messages. For revolutionary and ancient healing potions, visit nowalchemy.com.

I wish you all the blessings of this universe and beyond along your journey. May you realize your oneness with all living beings, open to healing from all afflictions this world may bestow upon you and discover your infinite abundance. Thank you for being here.

PHILIP LOVE 9/3/1947-11/4/2019

In honor of my father, Philip Love

Made in the USA
Coppell, TX
30 November 2020